Handling Experimental Data

WITHDRAWN

Handling Experimental Data

Mike Pentz and Milo Shott

Edited by Francis Aprahamian

Open University Press
Milton Keynes · Philadelphia

Open University Press
Celtic Court
22 Ballmoor
Buckingham MK18 1XW

and
1900 Frost Road, Suite 101
Bristol, PA 19007, USA

First published 1988
Reprinted 1989, 1992 (twice), 1994

British Library Cataloguing in Publication Data

Pentz, Mike
    Handling experimental data.
    1. Science. Experiments. Methodology
    I. Title   II. Shott, Milo
    507'.24

    ISBN 0-335-15897-8
    ISBN 0-335-15824-2 (pbk)

Library of Congress Cataloging-in-Publication Data

Pentz, Mike.
    Handling experimental data / Mike Pentz and Milo Shott; edited by
        Francis Aprahamian.
    p.   cm.
    Bibliography: p.
    Includes index.
    1. Science—Experiments—Observations.   2. Science—Experiments—Technique.
    I. Shott, Milo.   II. Aprahamian, Francis.   III. Title.
    Q182.3.P46   1988
    001.4'34—dc 19   88-6495

    ISBN 0-335-15897-8
    ISBN 0-335-15824-2 (pbk.)

Printed in Great Britain by
St Edmundsbury Press Limited, Bury St Edmunds, Suffolk

Contents

A note about the origins of this book

This book is an edited and amended version of the original material, published under the same title as an integral part of the Science Foundation Course of the Open University*. It is published for general use with the permission of the Open University's copyright office.

The aim and the level

The book attempts to introduce science students to basic principles and good practices in the collection, recording and evaluation of experimental data. Particular attention is paid to experimental errors and to the use of graphs in concise representation and interpretation of data. Only simple algebra and trigonometry are assumed and logarithms are introduced to illustrate the advantages of logarithmic graphs. No attempt is made to justify the statistical significance of standard deviations and standard errors on the mean, but examples are provided to illustrate their meanings.

All science students at the sixth-form and first-year tertiary levels will find this book useful.

* The Open University (1979) S101 *Science: A Foundation Course*, The Open University Press.

Introduction

Experiments and experimental data

The book is about *handling* experimental data, rather than about the design of experiments, but the two are closely related. *What* experimental data should be collected and then 'handled'? Is it worth while making hundreds of measurements of something or other, or will one or two do? How accurately should the measurements be made—will simple, relatively inaccurate measuring devices do, or are more sophisticated instruments needed?

Clearly, such questions about experimental design have a direct bearing on what data to collect and how to handle it, but they cannot be answered without reference to the *purpose* for which the experiment is being done. So before you start reading about the *handling* of experimental data it will be useful to spend a little time over the question: why do a particular experiment?

Consider the following (mostly imaginary) example: There was at one time a universal belief that heavier objects fell faster than lighter ones. This could be formulated as a *hypothesis*: if two objects of greatly differing weight are dropped together from a high tower (the leaning tower of Pisa perhaps?), the heavier one will reach the ground much sooner than the lighter one. Someone (Galileo perhaps?) wanted to do an experiment to *test this hypothesis*. What should he do? How should he design his experiment? Well, he would presumably take two objects of considerably different weight (e.g. 1 kg and 10 kg) to the top of the tower and then let them go, as nearly as possible, at the same time. Someone on the ground observes whether, as predicted by the hypothesis, the 10 kg object arrives appreciably before the 1 kg object. He is surprised to observe that the two objects arrive at pretty well the same time. So he probably shouts up to Galileo, 'Are you sure you released them at the same time? Maybe you'd better do it again!' And so Galileo does it again, with the same result. What can he say about the hypothesis he has set out to test by his experiment? You will probably agree that he could say, at the very least, that it looks very much as if the hypothesis is wrong. In this case a relatively simple experiment would suffice to *refute* this particular hypothesis.

But what if Galileo's experiment was meant to test a *different* hypothesis, namely that the acceleration, and hence the time of fall, of the two objects is *the same* whatever their weight? Would he now need to design his experiment differently?

He would clearly have to be much more concerned about the accuracy of his experimental data, and at the end of the day he could only say something like this: '*within the limits of accuracy of my measurements*, the two objects took the same time to fall to the ground, even though the one weighed about ten times as much as the other.' And, for this conclusion to have any practical significance, he would have to specify the limits of accuracy of his measurements, that is, he would have to say something about his estimated experimental errors. (In Sections 3 and 5 of this book you will find more detailed information about experimental errors and their significance in drawing conclusions from experiments.)

This example illustrates the general point that the design of an experiment, and particularly decisions about what data need to be obtained, and with what accuracy, depends upon what hypothesis the experiment is intended to test. Does this imply that *all* experiments are done to test some hypothesis? Aren't some experiments done in the spirit of open-ended enquiry: I wonder what will happen if ...? Of course they are. A scientist studying the behaviour of marmoset monkeys, for instance, might base an experiment on the question: 'I wonder what will happen to the adult behaviour of young marmosets if they are deprived of opportunities for play?' But it would be very surprising if the scientist didn't have some sort of hypothesis at the back of her mind, such as that deprivation of play opportunities might adversely affect mating abilities, for instance. And even where observations are made without any sort of hypothesis, explicit or implicit, they often provide the basis for the *subsequent* formulation of some hypothesis—indeed, this is often the main purpose of making the observations.

The practical conclusion to be drawn from this brief discussion of the question: *why am I doing this experiment?* is that the answer is likely to have an important influence on *how* the experiment should be done, and particularly on the quantity of the data to be obtained from the experiment and hence on what needs to be done to handle that data correctly.

1 Plans and records

1.1 Planning your experiments

The time available for performing an experiment is nearly always limited. It is important that you make the best use of your time, and to do this it is essential that you plan your work carefully. How should you do this? A research scientist would first specify, as precisely as possible, the aim of the experiment, and then make notes on the procedure to be followed and the measurements to be made. In teaching laboratories the notes are provided for you, and the aims of the experiments are stated. In most experiments you are also given an estimate of the time that you need to complete the experiment. You have to try to finish the experiment within that time.

First read the notes. You will then know which are the crucial measurements and which demand care. With this information you will not waste time by devoting unnecessary care to irrelevant measurements. For example—should that '20 ml' of reagent be measured accurately by pipette, or approximately by graduated cylinder, or will a rough visual estimate in a beaker suffice? Does it matter if the glassware in which it is measured is wet?

Many questions of this kind, and others that may occur to you while planning an experiment, can be answered by a preliminary experiment. It often pays to have a quick rehearsal before starting the experiment proper; it always pays to set up the apparatus to check that everything is functioning correctly. You will then have answers to questions like the following: What is the range over which measurements should be taken? What is a suitable interval between measurements? Where do the largest errors arise?

Once you have planned your experiment, it will be apparent which measurements require greatest care or repetition. You can also anticipate any periods when you are waiting for something to happen in the experiment. Use gaps in your experiment to calculate your results, to plot a graph as you go along, or perhaps to make preparations for the next experiment.

1.2 Keeping a laboratory notebook

Record your experiments in a notebook. You should write your comments, measurements and observations directly into it. It is bad practice to record anything on loose sheets of paper—they only get lost. To avoid confusion if you have to repeat an experiment, you should make a note of the date of your experiment. When you take readings, avoid doing mental arithmetic to record only a difference. For example, when weighing by difference, record both weighings so that you can check for mistakes.

When you are taking a set of readings, record them in a table, with each column headed correctly.

As an example, Table 1 shows the results of an experiment in which the extension of a copper wire was measured as a function of the load suspended from it.

TABLE 1   The extension of a copper wire

Mass kg	Extension mm
5	0.2
10	0.5
15	0.8
20	1.0
22.5	1.5
25	1.3
27.5	1.4
30	1.5
32.5	1.7
35.0	1.8
37.5	1.9
40.0	2.0
42.5	2.3
45.0	2.5
47.5	2.8
50.0	3.2

Notice that the table headings are written in a particular way:

$$\frac{mass}{kg} \quad and \quad \frac{extension}{mm}$$

This saves us the bother of having to write the units (e.g. kg) after each entry. We write mass/kg because an entry of 1 in the table is merely another way of saying

$$mass = 1\,kg$$

When both sides are divided by the units (kg), we get

$$\frac{mass}{kg} = 1$$

If you write a number incorrectly, do not overwrite it—there is always a danger of wrongly deciphering the overwritten number. Always cross out the wrong entry and record the correct number alongside it.

Remember that the unexpected observation may be the important one. Do not ignore it—write it down for easy reference.

Do not be afraid to spread your account over several pages. If your observations are set out clearly and well spaced, the time you save when referring to them will compensate handsomely for the paper used. It is never a waste of paper to jot down notes about the progress of your experiment or some observations, or to set out your measurements properly. It is remarkable how quickly a few cryptic numbers or comments, so self-explanatory when written, become utterly meaningless!

1.3 Hints on performing calculations

The advent of cheap electronic calculators has made life a great deal easier for scientists and science students! There is no longer any need to use cumbersome tables of logarithms, trigonometric functions, square roots, etc.

However, calculators bring their own problems; perhaps *because* they make the arithmetic so easy! The apparent infallibility of the calculator can lull you into an automatic acceptance of whatever answer is displayed, whereas, in fact, it is just as easy to make a mistake with the calculator as without it. So it is important to develop good habits when working with your calculator. You should find the hints we give below will save you a lot of time in the long run.

Get in the habit of checking calculations; it is very easy to make an error. You may have pressed the wrong key; you may have made a mistake in organizing the calculation; or the battery may be flat.

When checking, do not carry out the calculation in exactly the same way as you did the first time, otherwise you are likely to make the same mistake again. Take, for example, the expression:

$$K = \frac{2\pi \times 0.638 \times (27.1)^2 \times 1.28}{96.1} = 39.2$$

The first time, you could evaluate it in the order in which the numbers appear; the second time in reverse: i.e.

$$\frac{1.28 \times 27.1 \times 27.1 \times 0.638 \times \pi \times 2}{96.1}$$

Make a rough calculation to check whether the order of magnitude of your answer is right. To do this, round the numbers off so:

$$K \approx \frac{2 \times 3 \times (6 \times 10^{-1}) \times (30)^2 \times 1}{100} = \frac{36 \times 10^{-1} \times 9 \times 10^2}{10^2} \approx 30$$

A good way of diminishing the chance of error is to reduce the number of operations you have to do: avoid repeating the same operation several times if you can.

If you have to multiply or divide a series of numbers by a constant, make use of the constant factor facility on your calculator. For example, you might wish to calculate the values of energy E corresponding to a series of atomic spectral lines* whose frequencies f you know, using the formula:

$$E = hf$$

where h is a constant = 6.626×10^{-34} J s.

*Do not worry if you are not sure what atomic spectral lines are. Just think of E and f as being two variable quantities, connected by a constant h.

You should enter h on your calculator as a constant, which means that it can then be used to multiply the series of frequency values without the need to re-enter it. Not only will this reduce errors, it will save time. Since you will frequently have to multiply or divide a series of numbers by a constant factor, it is well worth while learning once and for all how to operate the constant factor key, rather than having to repeat the same key operations over and over again.

As a final check, look at your answer to make sure it is sensible.

Sometimes you will have no way of telling when a result is reasonable, but very often mistakes can be detected by asking a simple question (Was there really $96.75\,cm^3$ of water in that 200 ml beaker? Is the ratio of Mg atoms to O atoms in that compound likely to be 64.1?).

Finally a word about significant figures. All measurements are subject to inaccuracy: this means you can never quote an exact value for a measured physical quantity. If the mass of an object were estimated to lie somewhere between 3.75 g and 3.85 g, then the result would be quoted as 3.8 g. There would be no point in adding any figures to the right of the '8' as they are liable to be wrong. Such a measurement is said to have been made to two significant figures.

The same result could have been expressed in terms of kilograms, viz. 0.003 8 kg. The noughts to the right of the decimal point are necessary in order to establish the position of the decimal point relative to the digits '38'. The lack of figures to the right of the '8' still indicates that the accuracy of the determination is to two significant figures.

Suppose the same mass were expressed in milligrams; 3 800 mg. Once again the noughts are necessary in order to place the digits '38' relative to the decimal point (i.e. to indicate that we are now dealing with 3 thousand, 8 hundred). But now an element of uncertainty has crept in—are those noughts there only to indicate the position of the decimal point, or do they also mean that the measurement has been performed to an accuracy of four significant figures, i.e. the mass has been measured to lie between 3 799.5 mg and 3 800.5 mg? There is no way of telling unless an error is specifically quoted along with the measured value for example, $(3\,800 \pm 50)\,mg$. It is best to avoid the confusion by using an appropriate power of 10, that is: 3.8×10^3 mg for a determination to two significant figures; 3.800×10^3 mg to indicate four significant figures.

Of course, it would be more sensible in a case like this to express the mass in grams. The result would then be 3.8 g to two significant figures, or 3.800 g to four significant figures. It is usually a good idea to choose the units so as to be able to express the result with just one or two digits before the decimal point and without having to multiply by some power of 10. For example, a distance of 3 800 m, or 3.8×10^3 m, is more conveniently given as 3.8 km, and a length of 0.000 000 000 25 m, or 2.5×10^{-9} m, is more conveniently given as 2.5 nm. (See Section 6.5 for information about the multiples and fractions of standard units which can be used for this purpose.)

Always be on your guard against writing down a long string of digits that have no significance—it wastes your time and misleads others.

There is a strong temptation, when using a calculator, to present as a result, all the digits which the calculator displays (it seems somehow wasteful to discard what

appear to be perfectly good numbers!). *Resist this temptation*: even with sophisticated equipment, 8-digit accuracy is rarely achieved. Decide on the significance
limits of your measurements and quote your result *only* to the appropriate number
of figures.

Meaningless digits are particularly liable to arise from calculations. Suppose for
example that the lengths of four sticks are 0.46 cm, 27.6 cm, 3 cm and 0.12 cm,
what is the total length of the sticks when placed in a straight line end to end?

The sum of the lengths is:

$$
\begin{array}{r}
0.46 \\
27.6 \\
3 \\
0.12 \\
\hline
\text{Total} = 31.18
\end{array}
$$

But the length of the third stick is known only to the nearest centimetre, so the
sum is 31 cm, i.e. the accuracy of your final result is governed by the accuracy of
the quantity that you have measured least accurately.

To take a second example, suppose you know the radius of the Moon R_M to two
significant figures and you wish to use an expression of the type:

$$\text{distance to the Moon } d_M = 2R_M \times \frac{\text{distance to the eclipsing object}}{\text{diameter of the object}}$$

are you justified in quoting the moon's distance to eight figures? Say the figures
involved are

$$\frac{2(1\,500) \times 0.30}{1.70 \times 10^{-5}},$$

then the calculator display shows the number $5.294\,117\,6 \times 10^7$.

How would you report the result?

You are only justified in reporting it to two significant figures, i.e. as
5.3×10^7 m, because the diameter of the eclipsing object is known only to
two significant figures.

Or suppose that you use a balance that can weigh to within 0.01 g to determine
the mass (14.18 g) of element A that combines with a mass (1.20 g) of element B.
Using the known atomic masses of A and B, your calculator displays the ratio of
numbers of atoms of A and B as 4.003 377 8.

If this ratio were meaningful, it would give theoretical chemists
headaches—but is it?

No. It is meaningful only to three digits at best, and should therefore be
reported as 4.00, a value that is much more easily explained.

So the accuracy of a multiplication (or division) can be no better than that of the
least accurate quantity appearing as a factor.

(Some formulae involve factors that are pure numbers. For example, '2' and 'π' in
the factor 2π relating the circumference of a circle to its radius. For such

13

numbers there is, of course, no inaccuracy. Thus the single digit '2' implies '2.000 000 00 ...' and does not restrict the number of significant figures of the final result.)

Finally, just as it is meaningless to quote calculator displays to too many significant figures, when experimental accuracy is limited, it is even more dangerous to fall into an opposite trap of losing experimental accuracy by rounding-off the calculations too crudely.

For example, in an experiment with the diffraction of monochromatic light by a grating*, the angular position of the second order maximum is measured as $\theta = 45.2°$, by an instrument which is accurate to $\pm 0.1°$. You are told that the grating has 600 lines per mm and asked to calculate the wavelength λ of the diffracted light. The formula relating the quantities involved is

$$2\lambda = d \sin \theta \tag{1}$$

where d is the separation between two adjacent slits in the grating, i.e.

$$d = \frac{1 \text{ mm}}{600} \tag{2}$$

Your calculator tells you that

$$d = 1.666\,666\ 7 \times 10^{-6}\,\text{m}$$

$$\sin 45.2° = 0.709\,570\ 7$$

Is it reasonable to round-off these values to two significant figures ($d = 1.7 \times 10^{-6}\,\text{m}$, $\sin \theta = 0.71$) before substituting into equation 1?

Well, the answer is generally NO, even if in some particular case you may be lucky! The critical aspect is the experimental accuracy of the measurement of the diffraction angle θ, which is $\pm(1 \text{ in } 452) = \pm 2.212 \times 10^{-3} \approx 0.22$ per cent†. To round-off the value of d to two significant figures introduces a percentage error of

$$100 \times \frac{1.700\,000\,0 - 1.666\,666\ 7}{1.666\,666\ 7} = \frac{3.333\,3\ldots}{1.666\,6\ldots} = 2 \text{ per cent,}$$

which is an order of magnitude larger than the experimental error!

Rounding-off the value of $\sin \theta$ to two significant figures does not introduce a similarly large error in this particular case, simply because by chance the true value happens to be extremely close to the rounded-off value. The difference between 0.710 00 and 0.709 57 introduces a percentage error of only

$$100(0.710\,00 - 0.709\,57)/0.709\,57 \approx 0.06 \text{ per cent.}$$

---

*If you are a physics student, you will be familiar with this example. If you are not, it does not really matter. It is sufficient to appreciate that it involves a calculation of an *unknown* quantity on the basis of one *known* quantity (d) and one *measured* quantity (θ).

†As you can check for yourself, the corresponding error in $\sin \theta$ is very nearly the same (about 0.25 per cent).

As a general rule, to safeguard against the possibility of losing experimental accuracy by rough calculations, you could do worse than to refer to the Table 2.

TABLE 2   Significant figures in calculations.

Experimental accuracy	Minimum significant figures in calculations
10 per cent or worse	2
1 per cent to 10 per cent	3
0.1 per cent to 1 per cent	4

SAQ 1* Using the information about d and θ, given above, calculate the 'most likely' value of d and the limits within which it is accurate.

*SAQ stands for Self-Assessment Question. Its purpose is to help you to check whether you have properly understood something you have just been reading. You should try to work out your answer to each SAQ before referring to the SAQ answers and comments at the end of the book.

2 Errors

When scientists present the results of experimental measurements, they practically always specify a possible 'error' associated with the quoted results. Used in this context the word 'error' has a very specific meaning. It does *not* mean that the scientist made a mistake when doing the experiment; what it does mean is that—because of the inherent limitations of his equipment or of his measurement techniques—there will be some *uncertainty* associated with his final result. This uncertainty or 'error' conveys very significant information about the experiment and the result obtained and you will be expected to assess the errors in experiments that you perform. You will then be asked to quote your result together with your assessment of how much bigger and how much smaller it could possibly be, while still remaining consistent with the experiment you have performed. Such a result is usually then expressed in the form (50 ± 3) seconds, for example, and this is read as '50 plus or minus 3 seconds'. This means that your best estimate of the result is 50 seconds, but it could be as low as 47 seconds or as high as 53 seconds—you're uncertain by this amount. In the next Section, we shall discuss various types and sources of error, but first we shall give a few examples to illustrate *why* errors are so important.

(a) A chemist predicts about 7.0 kJ of energy will be released as heat in a certain chemical reaction. When the experiment is carried out, he finds that 6.5 kJ are released. Does the experiment disprove his theory? (1kJ = 1 kilojoule, see Section 6.)

Not necessarily; we have to ask what are the errors in the experiment. If the error was ± 1.0 kJ, then theory and experiment would be quite consistent, but if the error was only ± 0.1 kJ, then the theory would be disproved.

(b) Two experimenters measure the period of a pendulum. One quotes the result as (2.04 ± 0.03)s and the other as (1.94 ± 0.08)s. Do the two results contradict each other? Not really—they overlap, within their margins of error. In which result would you have most confidence? Obviously, the first. The quoted error is less than half that obtained by the second experimenter, which indicates a more careful measurement. We assume of course that the errors quoted are realistic!

(c) A biologist measures the wingspans of insects of a certain species that he has trapped at two locations, A and B. The mean wingspan of the insects from location A is 13.5 mm and the mean from location B is 12.0 mm. Can we conclude that insects from A definitely have a larger mean wingspan?

The answer is: No—not with the information provided. To draw any conclusion we need to know the possible error associated with the two mean values quoted. For instance, if the results were (13.5 ± 0.2) mm and (12.0 ± 0.2) mm then we would feel extremely confident that there was a significant difference between the insects at the two locations if we accepted the criteria in examples (a) and (b). However, populations of insects may vary quite a lot whereas the behaviour of pendulums and chemical reactions should be reproducible. We shall return to the problem of population later.

16

2.1 How do errors arise?

Errors, or uncertainties, in experimental results occur for a variety of reasons.

(a) *Mistakes!* First, let us dispose with human errors that are just silly blunders: misreading a scale, adding up the weights on a scale wrongly, recording a number wrongly, or making a mistake in a calculation. These are not really errors in the scientific sense at all. The best advice we can give you is 'don't make them'! Fortunately, mistakes like this generally show up if the measurements are repeated, and certainly all of them can be avoided by taking more care.

(b) *Human errors* There are human errors of a different kind, which are a reflection of the skill of the experimenter. For instance, parallax errors (Figure 1) can be counted in this class, as can the errors introduced by misaligning a measuring instrument or simply not setting it up as accurately as is possible. In general, all of these improve as one becomes more experienced at experimental work. Also modern instruments are designed to minimize such errors—for instance, meters with digital read out are now replacing ones with a needle and scale.

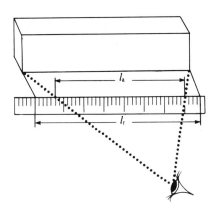

FIGURE 1   Parallax errors arising in the measurement of the length of an object. The apparent length, l_a in this case, is shorter than the real length, l_r, which would be measured if the ruler was placed in contact with the object.

(c) *Instrumental limitations* All measuring instruments have their limitations. Some are obvious, as in the case of some cheap wooden rulers, where one can see by eye that the divisions are not equally spaced. Others are not so apparent, but even the most expensive and sophisticated instrument will only be capable of measuring to a certain accuracy, and this is generally specified by its manufacturer. The manufacturer may also say that the specified accuracy will only be obtained under certain conditions; for example, a metal ruler may be calibrated at 20 °C, so that it becomes less accurate as the temperature deviates from 20 °C, owing to the expansion or contraction of the metal. However, the accuracy of the calibration of an instrument apart, there are generally limitations associated with the accuracy with which an observer can read a result. This will be determined partly by the fineness of the scale divisions, and partly by how well the observer can interpolate between scale divisions. Another important source of instrumental error arises from imperfect instruments, for example, friction in the balancing mechanism of a scale.

(d) *Errors caused by the act of observation* Examples include:

17

- animals (or people!) changing their behaviour while they are being observed, and this leading to a change in the quantity being measured,
- connecting a pressure gauge to a tyre and thereby causing a small drop in the pressure,
- a hot liquid cooling slightly when a cold thermometer is immersed in it.

(e) *Errors caused by extraneous influences* A variety of unwanted effects can cause errors in experiments. Draughts can lead to errors when weighing with a sensitive balance, impurities can cause errors in chemical experiments, and changes of temperature can lead to errors in many different experiments. Attempts should always be made to eliminate the effects, or at least to reduce them.

There are two more categories of error that we wish to discuss but, before we do so, let us make a few observations about measurements themselves. In general, measurements tend to fall into one of two categories. The first category is that where the quantity we are trying to measure has a well defined value. The aim is to find this value as precisely as possible. For example, measuring the length of a table, or the dimensions of a window pane, measuring the duration of a radio or TV programme, or measuring the mass of this booklet all fall into this category. On the other hand, quite a number of measurements attempt to quantify something that is not fixed. For instance, measuring the diameter of the Moon requires that the Moon be a perfect sphere. (Only then can we know what is meant by the term diameter.) Yet even though the Moon is not a perfect sphere, we insist on measuring its diameter. Of course, what we are really attempting to measure is its *mean* or average diameter—the diameter it would have if it were a perfect sphere. Furthermore, this can be very useful information, since deviations from this average value (provided that they are larger than any deviations due to the measuring techniques) can tell us something about the *real* shape of the Moon. Similarly the diameter of a piece of wire, or the thickness of a piece of paper, will probably vary from one position to another. So, if we want to substitute a value for one of these quantities into a formula of some kind, we must substitute the notional 'mean value'. That is the best we can do, and that is what most measurements are aiming to find. Perhaps more obvious is an attempt to measure the height of a twelve-year-old British child. Obviously no such quantity exists. But it could be very useful to know the mean-height of a twelve-year-old British child.

Now, measurements that are attempting to find the mean value of some quantity are subject to two other sorts of error: errors due to *statistical fluctuations*, and errors due to *unrepresentative samples*.

(f) *Errors due to statistical fluctuations* When we make measurements on a sample drawn from a large population, and try to deduce average properties of the population from these measurements, then we are likely to introduce errors. For example, suppose we measured the heights of one hundred twelve-year-old children. We would find a range of values for heights, and could calculate the average height for these children. If we repeated the experiment with another set of one hundred children, the average height would most likely be different. So, although measurements on a sample of one hundred children give us an *estimate* of what the average height of twelve-year-olds in the whole population is, it cannot be a precise result—there must be some uncertainty, some error associated with the fact that we have only taken a limited sample. As you might expect, the error in the estimate of the mean height of the population gets smaller as the size of the sample grows, but there will always be some statistical uncertainty as long as we are only measuring a selection from the complete population.

(g) *Errors due to use of unrepresentative samples* It is essential, when using a sample of measurements to deduce properties of a larger population, that the sample chosen is typical of the complete population. If we wanted to know the average height of twelve-year-old British children, then it would be wrong to measure just boys, it would be wrong to select children from just one location, and it would be wrong to select just children of coal miners.

Or, suppose a chemist wishes to find out the average amounts of various pollutants emerging from a chimney: if he makes his measurements at the same time each day, or always just after a furnace has been lit, then the results may not be a good indication of the average pollutant level. Designing a way of sampling in order to get results that are typical of the whole population can be extremely difficult, and any bias in the sample used can lead to errors in the results deduced.

2.2 Estimating the size of errors

Often one of the most difficult parts of an experiment is the estimation of the size of the errors involved. Obviously, no two experiments are exactly alike, so it is impossible to give hard and fast rules about how this should be done. However, we shall suggest an approach to this problem which you can use in most circumstances.

Is the result reproducible?

The first thing to ascertain is whether a measured value is reproducible. Usually, you should not be satisfied with a single measurement: repeat the measurement several times if possible. And, usually, you should reset the measuring instrument each time. If you are measuring the length of a rod, remove the ruler, reposition it, and read off the length again. When measuring the mean diameter of a wire with a screw-gauge, remove the gauge and reposition it to a different point on the circumference of the wire before taking another measurement. Or, suppose that you were measuring the rate of flow of water through a tube by collecting the emerging water for four minutes in a beaker and measuring the volume collected. You should repeat the collection of the water and the volume measurement a number of times. On the other hand, if you are weighing by difference, you should not reset the balance between weighings.

If the result is not reproducible ... random errors

In most cases (though not all), you will find that repeating measurements produces different results. This is because of random variations in the way that measuring instruments are set up; random variations in the way one interpolates the scale of an instrument; random variations in the quantity actually being measured; and so on. All measurements are subject to such *random errors*. The random error associated with any measurement determines the variability of the results, and the questions to ask are then: what is the best value of the quantity measured, and how do we deduce an error from the variability?

Taking the experiment of the rate of flow of water as an example, we shall assume that five measurements are made, and the volumes collected in four minutes are:

$$436.5\,cm^3 \qquad 437.5\,cm^3 \qquad 435.9\,cm^3 \qquad 436.2\,cm^3 \qquad 436.9\,cm^3$$

Assuming that there is nothing to choose between these measurements (i.e. they were all taken with the same care and skill, and with the same measuring instruments), then the best estimate of the water volume is the average, or mean, value, of the five readings. If we represent the volume by V, then we usually represent the average volume by $\bar{V}$. The bar over the V just means 'average value', and $\bar{V}$ can just be read as 'the average value of V'. So the best estimate of the volume is:

$$\bar{V} = \frac{(436.5 + 437.5 + 435.9 + 436.2 + 436.9)\,cm^3}{5}$$

$$= 436.6\,cm^3$$

Now, what error should we associate with this value? The measurements are spread out between $435.9\,cm^3$ and $437.5\,cm^3$, which is from $(436.6 - 0.7)\,cm^3$ to $(436.6 + 0.9)\,cm^3$. If we average the negative and positive deviations, then we can say that the *spread* is about $\pm 0.8\,cm^3$. However, the volume is unlikely to lie right at the ends of this spread, so quoting an error of $\pm 0.8\,cm^3$ would be unduly pessimistic. As a rough rule of thumb, we generally take the error as about 2/3 of the spread, so in this case the error is about $\pm 0.5\,cm^3$. Note that this is only a rough rule of thumb, and it still overestimates the error in the mean value, particularly when a large number of measurements are taken. In a later Section, we shall show how better estimates of errors can be obtained. *However, in many situations, the simple procedure is adequate and we recommend its use.*

You will appreciate that if one reading was very different from all of the others, then determining the likely error from the spread would be misleadingly pessimistic. Common sense would suggest that the odd reading is ignored when calculating the mean and the error, and possibly that a few more measurements are taken. For example, if the last reading for the volume were $432.9\,cm^3$ rather than $436.9\,cm^3$, then it would be wise to ignore it, provided you can be sure that nothing has changed in the conditions of the experiment.

In the example we have discussed, the variability in the measured values of V could arise from the combination of a number of factors. These include actual variations in the flow rate, errors in timing four minutes, inserting and removing the beaker to collect the water too early or too late, and inaccuracies in measuring the volume collected. The beauty of repeating the measurements is that we get an overall measure of the random errors involved, and it isn't necessary to assess the individual contributions.

If the result is reproducible ...

You will find when repeating some experimental measurements that you record exactly the same result each time. Does this then mean that there is *no* error associated with the measurement? In most cases, it certainly does not. To take a simple example again, assume that the results of measuring the length of a bar five times were:

73 mm   73 mm   73 mm   73 mm   73 mm

i.e. five identical readings. Here we can deduce the error from the number of significant figures recorded. By writing down 73 mm, the experimenter is implicitly recording that the length is closer to 73 mm than it is to 72 mm or to 74 mm, or that the length lies between 72.5 mm and 73.5 mm. The error is therefore ± 0.5 mm, and the result should be quoted as (73 ± 0.5) mm. Of course, this uncertainty has resulted from the limitations of his measuring equipment. This is a lesson you should take to heart. One of the first things you should do when you use a piece of equipment is assess the inherent limitations of the equipment itself.

(a)

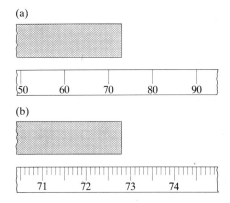

(b)

FIGURE 2   The scale in (a) can be read to the nearest 1 mm, but the scale in (b) to the nearest 0.1 mm.

Naturally, in situations such as this, where identical readings are obtained, it is particularly important to make sure that you are reading the instrument as precisely as possible. With the scale shown in Figure 2a, the quoted results are the best that can be expected. However, the scale shown in Figure 2b can be read more accurately—a value of 72.8 mm could be recorded in this case. A set of repeated measurements might then show some variability from which the likely error could be deduced. Of course, if repeated measurements all came up with the result 72.8 mm, then we would have to conclude that the error was ± 0.05 mm.

Systematic errors

It is fairly easy to assess the size of the random errors that we have been discussing. Averaging a number of readings tends to cancel out the effects of such errors, and the spread of the readings allows us to estimate the size of the random errors involved. Unfortunately there are other types of error—known as *systematic errors*—the effects of which are much more difficult to assess. Systematic errors are errors that *systematically* shift the measurements in one direction away from the true value. Thus repeated readings do not show up the presence of systematic errors, and no amount of averaging will reduce their effects. Both systematic and random errors are often present in the same measurement, and the different effects they have are contrasted in Figure 3.

Many systematic errors arise from the measuring instrument used. For example, a meter rule may in fact be 1.005 m long, so that all measurements made with it are systematically $\frac{1}{2}$ per cent too short. Or the rule may have 0.1 mm worn from one

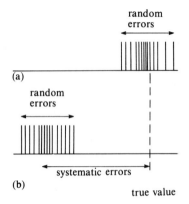

random
errors

(a)

random
errors

systematic errors

(b)

true value

FIGURE 3   (a) random errors alone lead to a spread of measurements about the true value.

(b)   Systematic errors lead to a displacement of the measurements, and when random errors are present as well, the measurements are not spread about the true value.

end, so that all lengths measured systematically appear 0.1 mm longer than they are. Systematic errors like these in instruments can often only be discovered and estimated by comparison with a more accurate and reliable instrument, and this should be done wherever possible. If this is done, the effects of these errors can be eliminated by correcting the measured results.

The experimenter himself may introduce systematic errors into an experiment. In timing ten swings of a pendulum he might tend to start the stopwatch late and stop it too early, so that the measured period is too short. Such errors can best be detected by changing the way in which the experiment is done: the timing error would show up if, for example, twenty swings of the pendulum were also timed.

Systematic errors can also arise for the reasons noted in Section 2.1 (d), (e) and (g). These errors are associated with the observation affecting the measurement, with extraneous influences affecting the measurement, and with unrepresentative samples. In general, extra experiments are needed to check for the presence of such errors.

Undoubtedly systematic errors are more difficult to deal with than random errors. Your ability to cope with them will certainly improve as you gain experience of experimental work. But bear in mind that, time and again, experimenters—often very distinguished and experienced ones—have produced results that disagree; almost always the difference has been traced to one (or more!) of them having seriously misjudged or overlooked a systematic error. The moral therefore is that when you produce a result that conflicts with another result, or a theoretical prediction, you should carefully examine your experiment to reassess all systematic errors.

2.3   Combining errors

In the majority of experiments, there is more than one source of error. For instance, several random and systematic errors may be present in measurements of a single quantity. Furthermore, it is quite likely that a number of measurements of different quantities (each of which has an error associated with it) will have to be combined to calculate the required result. So it is important to know how errors are combined to get the overall error in an experiment.

Since we do not want to get involved here with statistical theories, we shall not prove the various results that will be presented. However, we shall make some attempts to justify that they are reasonable. Our only objective here is that you should be able to use the appropriate result in various experimental situations that you meet.

2.3.1   Combining errors in a single quantity

We have already stressed the need to make a series of measurements in order to determine the random errors involved in an experiment. But there may also be one, or more, systematic errors involved, which will contribute to the overall error in the experiment.

It is important to distinguish between such systematic errors that you can identify and allow for—and which, therefore, will *not* contribute to the error in the final result—and systematic errors for which you can only say that they are 'likely to be $\pm x'$. For example, in the water flow experiment discussed in Section 2.2, the two different kinds of systematic error could occur in timing the four-minute interval. It could be that the stopwatch runs slow; comparing it with the telephone talking clock might show that it lost 10 s every hour, which is equivalent to (10/15) s in 240 s (i.e. 4 minutes). To allow for this error, we would multiply the volumes collected by the factor (240–10/15)/240, and this would mean that the slow running of the watch did not contribute an error to the final answer. The calibration procedure eliminates the error. However, we might have a tendency to start or stop the stop watch too early or too late each time. We don't *know* that such a systematic error is present, but it is certainly possible. A reasonable estimate for the possible size of such an error is ± 0.2 s—anything longer would probably be detected. This error of ± 0.2 s in 240 s, or ± 1 part in 1 200, would lead to an error of ± 1 part in 1 200 in the volume of water collected. As the average volume of water collected was 436.6 cm^3, this would lead to an error of: ± 436.6 cm^3/1 200 $= \pm 0.4$ cm^3.

So the difference between these two types of systematic error is that we know that one is definitely present, and we can measure and correct for its effect, whereas the other may or may not be present, and we can only make an educated guess at its possible magnitude. Essentially, once we have identified, measured and corrected for the first type of error, it ceases to be a source of error in the final result.

Returning to the problem of combining errors, how do we combine a systematic error of ± 0.4 cm^3 arising from the timing with a random error in the volume of water collected of ± 0.5cm^3? The obvious answer would seem to be to add them directly to get a total error of 0.5 cm^3 + 0.4 cm^3 = 0.9 cm^3, but this is really being unduly pessimistic. Since the random error and the systematic error are entirely *independent*, it is highly unlikely (though possible, of course) that both errors will have their maximum positive error or their maximum negative error. There will generally be a partial cancellation, and this should be allowed for. The rule for combining two independent errors in the same quantity, and we stress that it only applies if the errors are independent, is:

$$E = \sqrt{(e_1^2 + e_2^2)}$$

where E is the overall error, and e_1, e_2 are the individual errors that are to be combined. Thus, in the water-flow example,

$$E = \sqrt{(0.5\,\text{cm}^3)^2 + (0.4\,\text{cm}^3)^2}$$
$$= \sqrt{0.25\,\text{cm}^6 + 0.16\,\text{cm}^6}$$
$$= \sqrt{0.41\,\text{cm}^6}$$
$$= 0.6\,\text{cm}^3$$

This is obviously larger than either of the contributing errors, but considerably smaller than their sum.

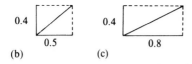

FIGURE 4   Adding lines: (a) in the same direction, and (b) and (c) in independent directions.

You may find that the following argument justifying this procedure helps you to remember the result. We can represent the individual errors by lines that have lengths proportional to the size of the error. Direct addition can then be represented by putting two lines together in the way shown in Figure 4a to produce a line equal to their sum. However, since the errors are independent, we need to add these lines in some way that preserves their independence. This can be done if we arrange the lines at right angles, as in Figure 4b, and take their sum as being the diagonal of the rectangle. (This is, in fact, the way we add forces that are acting in different directions.) Changing one 'error' now has no effect in the direction of the other, as you can see in Figure 4c. The length of the diagonal is just given by Pythagoras' theorem,

i.e.
$$(\text{diagonal})^2 = 0.5^2 + 0.4^2$$
$$\text{diagonal} = \sqrt{0.5^2 + 0.4^2} = 0.6$$

If more than two errors are involved, the method is still the same in principle. Suppose that we think that there may be a systematic error of $\pm 0.3\,\text{cm}^3$ in measuring the volume of water collected. Then the overall error is:

$$E = \sqrt{(0.5\,\text{cm}^3)^2 + (0.4\,\text{cm}^3)^2 + (0.3\,\text{cm}^3)^2}$$
$$= 0.7\,\text{cm}^3$$

which is, again, larger than the individual errors, but smaller than their sum.

When errors are not independent, they are much more difficult to deal with, unless the form of the dependence is known precisely. Because of their dependence, a large positive error from one source may always result in a large negative error from another source, thus causing cancellation and an overall error that is much smaller than the individual errors. Or, alternatively, a positive error may always result in a positive error, so that the overall error is more like the sum of the individual errors. No precise rules can be given for dealing with dependent errors, and we only expect you to be aware of this problem.

To summarize:

> independent errors $e_1, e_2, e_3, \ldots$ in a measured quantity will give rise to an overall error E given by:
>
> $$E = \sqrt{(e_1^2 + e_2^2 + e_3^2 + \ldots)}$$

2.3.2 Combining errors in sums, differences, products, ratios and powers

In the last Section, we were concerned with combining errors in a *single measured quantity* to find the total error in that quantity. Often, however, the aim of an experiment is to evaluate something that depends on *several measured quantities*, each of which has its own total error. In this Section, we simply state the rules that apply to various combinations of quantities and provide a few examples of how to use them. You do not need to memorize any of the rules; you just need to recognize which one applies to the situation you encounter.

As an example, suppose that you want to know the difference in temperature of something before and after some event has occurred, i.e. you may want to evaluate $T = T_1 - T_2$ having measured T_1 and T_2 independently. How is the error in T related to the overall errors in T_1 and T_2 ?

You simply select the appropriate equation from Box 1 (p. 27), which gives the basic rules that apply in such situations. For the difference in two quantities, you would use equation 3.

Note that percentage errors can be used in place of fractional errors in the equations of Box 1. Take equation 4, for example. The percentage error in X is related to the fractional error $\Delta X / X$ in the following way:

$$\text{percentage error in } X = \frac{\Delta X}{X} \times 100$$

this is just the definition of a percentage. So:

percentage error in X

$$= \frac{\Delta X}{X} \times 100$$

$$= 100 \sqrt{\left(\frac{\Delta A}{A}\right)^2 + \left(\frac{\Delta B}{B}\right)^2}$$

$$= \sqrt{10^4 \left[\left(\frac{\Delta A}{A}\right)^2 + \left(\frac{\Delta B}{B}\right)^2\right]}$$

$$= \sqrt{\left(100 \frac{\Delta A}{A}\right)^2 + \left(100 \frac{\Delta B}{B}\right)^2}$$

$$= \sqrt{(\text{percentage error in } A)^2 + (\text{percentage error in } B)^2}$$

25

Again, you are not expected to understand the statistical theory which leads to these results, nor are you expected to remember them. You should regard them as recipes, refer to them, and apply them, as necessary. The numerical examples which follow will illustrate how the rules should be applied.

Example 1

An object is made from two parts. One part has mass $M_1 = (120 \pm 5)\,\text{kg}$ and the other has mass $M_2 = (90 \pm 3)\,\text{kg}$. What is the total mass M, and the error ΔM in this mass?

$$M = (M_1 + M_2) \pm \Delta M$$

$$= 120\,\text{kg} + 90\,\text{kg} \pm \Delta M$$

$$= 210\,\text{kg} \pm \Delta M$$

Since we are dealing with the error in a sum, we use equation 3 in **Box 1**:

$$\Delta M = \sqrt{(\Delta M_1)^2 + (\Delta M_2)^2}$$

$$= \sqrt{(5\,\text{kg})^2 + (3\,\text{kg})^2}$$

$$= \sqrt{25\,\text{kg}^2 + 9\,\text{kg}^2}$$

$$= \sqrt{34\,\text{kg}^2}$$

$$= 6\,\text{kg}$$

So the total mass is $(210 \pm 6)\,\text{kg}$.

Comment   The total error is larger than either of the contributing errors, but not as large as their sum. This is because we have assumed that the errors in the masses are independent so that some partial cancellation is expected to occur.

Example 2

The temperature in a room before a heater is switched on is $(16.2 \pm 0.4)\,°\text{C}$, and one hour after the the heater is switched on it is $(22.7 \pm 0.4)\,°\text{C}$. What is the temperature rise T?

$$T = (T_1 - T_2) \pm \Delta T$$

$$= (22.7 - 16.2)\,°\text{C} \pm \Delta T$$

$$= 6.5\,°\text{C} \pm \Delta T$$

Since we need to find the error in the difference between two quantities, we again use equation 3 in **Box 1**:

$$\Delta T = \sqrt{(\Delta T_1)^2 + (\Delta T_2)^2}$$

$$= \sqrt{(0.4\,°\text{C})^2 + (0.4\,°\text{C})^2}$$

$$= 0.6\,°\text{C}$$

So we can quote the temperature difference as:

$$T = (6.5 \pm 0.6)°\text{C}$$

Comment   The error in the difference is *not* equal to the difference between the

Box 1*

Assuming that independent measurements A and B, which have total errors ΔA and ΔB associated with them, are combined to give the result X, which has error ΔX then:

$$\left.\begin{array}{l} \text{if} \quad X = A + B \\ \text{or} \quad X = A - B \end{array}\right\} \longrightarrow \Delta X = \sqrt{(\Delta A)^2 + (\Delta B)^2} \qquad (3)$$

(notice that only a plus sign appears in the expression for ΔX because errors in A and B increase ΔX regardless of whether X is the sum of or difference in A and B.)

$$\left.\begin{array}{l} \text{if} \quad X = AB \\ \text{or} \quad X = A/B \end{array}\right\} \longrightarrow \frac{\Delta X}{X} = \sqrt{\left(\frac{\Delta A}{A}\right)^2 + \left(\frac{\Delta B}{B}\right)^2} \qquad (4)$$

$$\text{if} \quad X = A^n \longrightarrow \frac{\Delta X}{X} = n \frac{\Delta A}{A} \qquad (5)$$

If a constant k, which has no error associated with it, is involved, then:

$$\text{if} \quad X = kA \quad \Delta X = k\Delta A \qquad (6)$$

$$\text{but also} \quad \frac{\Delta X}{X} = \frac{\Delta A}{A} \qquad (7)$$

(so the constant has *no* effect on the fractional error)

$$\left.\begin{array}{l} \text{if} \quad X = kA + B \\ \text{or} \quad X = kA - B \end{array}\right\} \longrightarrow \Delta X = \sqrt{(k\Delta A)^2 + (\Delta B)^2} \qquad (8)$$

$$\left.\begin{array}{l} \text{if} \quad X = kAB \\ \text{of} \quad X = kA/B \end{array}\right\} \longrightarrow \frac{\Delta X}{X} = \sqrt{\left(\frac{\Delta A}{A}\right)^2 + \left(\frac{\Delta B}{B}\right)^2} \qquad (9)$$

$$\text{if} \quad X = kA^n \longrightarrow \frac{\Delta X}{X} = n \frac{\Delta A}{A} \qquad (10)$$

When more than two quantities are involved, the equations are extended in a straightforward way:

If $X = A + B - C + D \cdots \longrightarrow$

$$\Delta X = \sqrt{(\Delta A)^2 + (\Delta B)^2 + (\Delta C)^2 + (\Delta D)^2 \cdots} \qquad (11)$$

(notice again that only plus signs appear under the square root)

If $X = \dfrac{A \times B}{C \times D} \longrightarrow$

$$\frac{\Delta X}{X} = \sqrt{\left(\frac{\Delta A}{A}\right)^2 + \left(\frac{\Delta B}{B}\right)^2 + \left(\frac{\Delta C}{C}\right)^2 + \left(\frac{\Delta D}{D}\right)^2} \qquad (12)$$

(again note that only plus signs appear under the square root)

*You may wonder why *actual* errors ΔA, ΔB are combined for sums and differences and why *fractional* (percentage) errors must be combined for products and ratios. The reason is simple: sums and differences always involve only values of *the same* physical quantity, e.g. length, mass or time. Different quantities cannot be added or subtracted. However, many physical quantities are defined as products or ratios of two *different* quantities—for example, speed is distance divided by time. Here actual errors cannot be combined, because they have different dimensions. Instead we combine fractional or percentage errors, which are just dimensionless numbers, which can be added.

errors, or even to the square root of the difference between the squares of the two errors. Even when subtracting two quantities the resulting error must be *larger* than either of the individual errors.

Example 3

The speed v of a train is measured as $(80 \pm 5)\,\text{km hr}^{-1}$ over a measured time t of (0.20 ± 0.02) hours. What distance x does the train travel in this time?

$$\text{Distance } x = \text{speed } v \times \text{time } t$$

$$= (80\,\text{km hr}^{-1} \times 0.20\,\text{hr}) \pm \Delta x$$

$$= 16\,\text{km} \pm \Delta x$$

In this case, we are using a product of two physically different quantities to calculate the distance, so the error Δx must be calculated from equation 4 in Box 1, using the fractional errors of each quantity:

$$\frac{\Delta x}{x} = \sqrt{\left(\frac{\Delta v}{v}\right)^2 + \left(\frac{\Delta t}{t}\right)^2}$$

$$\frac{\Delta x}{16\,\text{km}} = \sqrt{\left(\frac{5\,\text{km hr}^{-1}}{80\,\text{km hr}^{-1}}\right)^2 + \left(\frac{0.02\,\text{hr}}{0.20\,\text{hr}}\right)^2}$$

$$= \sqrt{3.9 \times 10^{-3} + 10^{-2}}$$

$$= 0.12$$

$$\Delta x = 0.12 \times 16\,\text{km} \approx 2\,\text{km}$$

The result is, therefore: $\qquad x = (16 \pm 2)\,\text{km}$

Comment When dealing with products (and with ratios and powers), *fractional errors* are used—we cannot use the same expression as for sums and differences. Lets see what would happen if we were to try.

Suppose $\qquad \Delta x = \sqrt{(\Delta v)^2 + (\Delta t)^2}$

i.e. $\qquad \Delta x = \sqrt{(5\,\text{km hr}^{-1})^2 + (0.02\,\text{hr})^2}$

Clearly, this equation is crazy: how do we add a square of speed to a square of time? The use of fractional errors reduces all contributing errors to dimensionless ratios, which can be combined.

Example 4

A mass of $(1.00 \pm 0.01)\,\text{g}$ of aluminium (symbol Al) reacts with a mass of $(8.88 \pm 0.01)\,\text{g}$ of bromine (symbol Br). What is the value of n in the formula of the product, AlBr_n?

The value of n is: $\qquad n = \dfrac{\text{moles of bromine}}{\text{moles of aluminium}}$

$$\text{moles of Br} = \frac{\text{mass of Br}}{\text{relative atomic mass Br}} = \frac{(8.88 \pm 0.01)\,\text{g}}{79.90\,\text{g mol}^{-1}}$$

$$\text{moles of Al} = \frac{\text{mass of Al}}{\text{relative atomic mass Al}} = \frac{(1.00 \pm 0.01)\,\text{g}}{26.98\,\text{g mol}^{-1}}$$

$$n = \frac{8.88\ \text{g}}{79.90\ \text{g mol}^{-1}} \div \frac{1.00\ \text{g}}{26.98\ \text{g mol}^{-1}} \pm \Delta n$$

$$= 3.00 \pm \Delta n$$

Since we use a ratio to calculate n, we must use equation 4 in the box to calculate Δn. Also, since the relative atomic masses are constants, they do not change the *fractional* errors (see equation 9 in Box 1), and we need to worry only about the errors in the masses:

$$\frac{\Delta n}{n} = \left[\left(\frac{\Delta m_{Br}}{m_{Br}}\right)^2 + \left(\frac{\Delta m_{Al}}{m_{Al}}\right)^2\right]^{1/2}$$

$$= \left[\left(\frac{0.01\ \text{g}}{8.88\ \text{g}}\right)^2 + \left(\frac{0.01\ \text{g}}{1\ \text{g}}\right)^2\right]^{1/2}$$

$$= (1.3 \times 10^{-6} + 100 \times 10^{-6})^{1/2}$$

$$= 0.01$$

So the value of n is 3.00 ± 0.03.

Comment The fractional error in one mass (of Br) is about a tenth of the fractional error in the other mass (of Al). The result is that the fractional error in n is very nearly equal to the fractional error in the mass of Al. When two fractional errors are combined the larger one is often dominant because they are squared in equations 4, 8 and 9. So if you notice that one fractional error is about a third (or less) of another, you can ignore the smaller one.

Example 5

The diameter of a sphere is measured to be $(7.2 \pm 0.5)\,\text{cm}$. What is its volume?

$$\text{Volume of a sphere, } V = \frac{\pi d^3}{6}$$

$$= \frac{\pi}{6}\,(7.2\ \text{cm})^3$$

$$= 1.95 \times 10^2\ \text{cm}^3$$

Now $\pi/6$ is a constant, so it doesn't change the *fractional* error (see equation 7 in Box 1), and we only need to worry about the error in d^3. Using equation 10 in Box 1,

$$\frac{\Delta V}{V} = \frac{3\Delta d}{d}$$

$$= \frac{3 \times 0.5\ \text{cm}}{7.2\ \text{cm}} = 0.21$$

$$\Delta V = 0.21 \times (1.95 \times 10^2\ \text{cm}^3)$$

$$= 41\ \text{cm}^3$$

So the volume is:

$$V = (2.0 \pm 0.4) \times 10^2\ \text{cm}^3$$

Comment   The fractional error in the volume is *three times* larger than the fractional error in the measured diameter. Because errors increase so rapidly when powers are taken, you should always take particular care to reduce errors when measuring quantities that will be raised to some power. Note also that it would be *wrong* to reason that since:

$$V = \frac{\pi}{3} \times d \times d \times d$$

then

$$\frac{\Delta V}{V} = \sqrt{\frac{\Delta d^2}{d} + \frac{\Delta d^2}{d} + \frac{\Delta d^2}{d}}$$

$$= \sqrt{3} \frac{\Delta d}{d}$$

The equation for the error in a product *cannot* be used in this case, because the three terms that have to be multiplied are exactly the same—and therefore certainly not independent.

2.4   Miscellaneous tips about errors

Don't worry about errors in the errors!   Errors, by their very nature, cannot be precisely quantified. So a statement like $l = (2.732 \pm 0.312)$ m is rather silly, and the result should be quoted as $l = (2.7 \pm 0.3)$ m. As a general rule:

> Errors should usually be quoted only to one significant figure; two significant figures are sometimes justified, particularly if the first figure is a 1.

You should bear this in mind when trying to assess the magnitude of errors, and when doing calculations involving errors. Don't be concerned about 30 per cent errors in your errors—they really don't matter.

Neglecting small errors   As you have seen in Example 4, the total error in a result may be a combination of several contributing errors, and these contributing errors may have widely varying sizes. But, because the errors (or fractional errors) combine as the sum of the squares, as a general rule:

> When calculating errors in *sums and differences*, ignore any errors that are less than 1/3 of the largest error, and when calculating errors in *products and ratios*, ignore any *fractional* error that is less than 1/3 of the largest error.

Concentrate on reducing the dominant errors   As we have just shown, the largest errors will dominate the error in the final result, and small errors can often be neglected. It is therefore very important when doing experiments not to waste a lot of time reducing small errors when much larger errors are also present. Using Example 4, any time spent trying to reduce the error of ± 0.01 g in the mass of bromine would be wasted as long as there is an error of ± 0.01 g in the mass of aluminium, which is 10 times larger in fractional terms. As a general rule:

> Find out as early as possible in an experiment what the dominant errors are, and then concentrate your time and effort on reducing them (if the precision of your experiment is not sufficient for your purpose).

Take care when differences and powers are involved Suppose that you measure two angles in an experiment, $\theta_1 = (73 \pm 3)$ degrees and $\theta_2 = (65 \pm 3)$ degrees, and calculate the difference, i.e. $\theta = \theta_1 - \theta_2 = 8$ degrees. The error is:

$$\Delta\theta = \sqrt{(\Delta\theta_1)^2 + (\Delta\theta_2)^2}$$
$$= \sqrt{3^2 + 3^2} \approx 4 \text{ degrees}$$

So $\theta = (8 \pm 4)$ degrees. This is a 50 per cent error compared with only about 4 per cent in the individual measurements!

On the other hand, suppose you measure an edge of a cube as $l = (6.0 \pm 0.5$ mm), and then calculate the volume: $V = 36$ mm^3. The error is given by:

$$\frac{\Delta V}{V} = \frac{3 \, \Delta l}{l} = \frac{3 \times 0.5}{6} = 0.25$$

The fractional error in the volume is three times greater than in the length measurement. As a general rule:

> If calculating the result of an experiment involves taking the difference between two nearly equal measured quantities, or taking the power of a measured quantity, then pay particular attention to reducing the errors in those quantities.

3 Graphs

3.1 Graphs: why use them?

Graphs are frequently used to represent the results of experiments, and some of the reasons for their use should become clear if you compare Table 1 (repeated from Section 1) with Figure 5. The Table and the graph both summarize the results obtained in an experiment in which the extension of a copper wire is measured as a function of the load suspended from it.

TABLE 1   The extension of a copper wire

Mass kg	Extension mm
5	0.2
10	0.5
15	0.8
20	1.0
22.5	1.5
25	1.3
27.5	1.4
30	1.5
32.5	1.7
35.0	1.8
37.5	1.9
40.0	2.0
42.5	2.3
45.0	2.5
47.5	2.8
50.0	3.2

After glancing at the graph you can say:

(a) For extensions up to about 2.1 mm, the extension is proportional to the mass, i.e. doubling the mass produces twice the extension.

(b) For extensions greater than about 2.1 mm, the wire extends more easily, and extension is no longer proportional to mass. (In fact, if the wire is extended more than 2.1 mm, it will not return to its original length when the load is removed, and this extension is called the *elastic limit*.)

(c) The points lie fairly close to the straight line (with one exception), and the errors, or uncertainties, in the experimental measurements must be about ± 0.05 mm in the extension, and/or ± 1 kg in the mass.

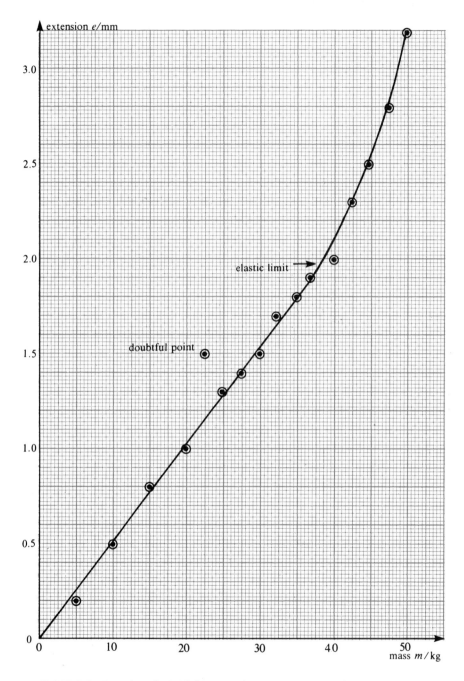

FIGURE 5 Extension of a loaded copper wire.

(d) The point plotted as extension 1.5 mm, mass 22.5 kg is anomalous—it is much farther from the line than any other point, in fact higher than the next two larger masses, and ought to be checked.

(e)   The extension that you would expect for a mass of 25 kg is smaller than the measured 1.3 mm, but probably nearer 1.25 mm. The straight line drawn *averages* out experimental errors in individual measurements.

(f)   The extension that you would expect for a mass of 22 kg is 1.1 mm. In this case the straight line on the graph is used to *interpolate* between measured values.

(g)   The gradient of the line relating extension e to mass m is 2.04 mm/40 kg = 0.051 mm kg^{-1} and the intercept is zero. The equation describing the relationship between e and m is:

$$e = 0.051 \text{ mm kg}^{-1} \times m$$

We shall discuss gradients of graphs in more detail in Section 3.4

All of the statements (a)–(g) could be made by examining the data in Table 4—after all, the graph was plotted using only the information in the Table. However, it would take a long time to arrive at (a)–(g) from the tabulated information, whereas they can all be very rapidly deduced from the graph. This is the great advantage of graphs as visual aids. The form of the relationship between measured quantities, the typical errors in measurements and the presence of anomalous measurements are readily apparent, and graphs allow straightforward averaging of experimental measurements, interpolation between measurements and (in simple cases) determination of the equation relating measured quantities.

3.2   Graphs: how to plot them

(a)   *Label both axes to show what quantity is plotted*   Since only pure numbers can be plotted, the quantity measured must be divided by its units before plotting. This means that the axis should be labelled *quantity/units*. Thus, in Figure 5, the axes are labelled extension e/mm, and mass m/kg. The doubtful point has coordinates (1.5, 22.5) and, using the labelling on the axes, we interpret this as:

$$\frac{\text{extension } e}{\text{mm}} = 1.5 \qquad \frac{\text{mass } m}{\text{kg}} = 22.5$$

or extension e = 1.5 mm, mass m = 22.5 kg.

(b)   *Choose the scales on the axes to make plotting simple*   Generally this means letting 10 small divisions on the graph paper equal 1, 2, 5, or some multiple of 10 of these numbers. Do not make your life difficult by making 10 small divisions equal 3 or 7; you would take much longer to plot the graph, and the chances of misplotting points would be very much higher.

(c)   *Choose the range of the scales on the axes so that the points are suitably spread out on the graph paper*, and not all cramped into one corner. In some cases this may mean excluding zero from the axis: for example, if lengths measured in an experiment varied between 5.2 m and 7.7 m, it would be better to allow the scale to run from 5 m to 8 m as in Figure 6a rather than from zero to 8 m as in Figure 6b.

(d) *Plot the independent variable along the horizontal axis and the dependent variable along the vertical axis* For example, to obtain the results shown in Figure 5, various masses were hung from the wire and the resulting extension was measured. The mass is the independent variable and is plotted horizontally, the extension is the dependent variable and is plotted vertically, and Figure 5 shows how the extension of the wire *depends* on the mass hung from it.

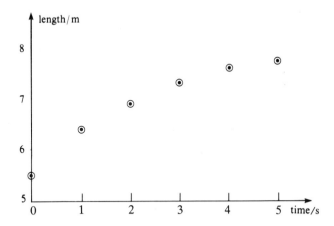

FIGURE 6   (a)   Sensible choice of scale.

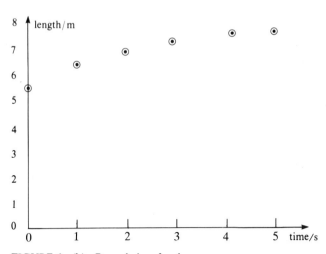

FIGURE 6   (b)   Poor choice of scale.

(e) *Plot results clearly* Tiny dots may be confused with dirt on the graph paper, and big dots give loss of precision. Either crosses (X) or dots with circles round them (⊙) are preferable.

(f) *When taking readings, generally spread them out evenly* over the range of values of the quantity measured. Figure 7a is poor, Figure 7b is better. An

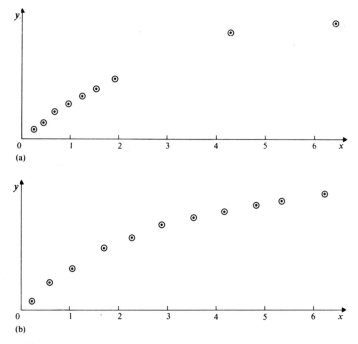

(a)

(b)

FIGURE 7   (a)   Readings unevenly spread.   (b)   Readings evenly spread.

exception to this rule is when you want to measure an intercept—then it is desirable to have a few extra points close to the axis (as shown in Figure 8)—or when the graph is changing shape.

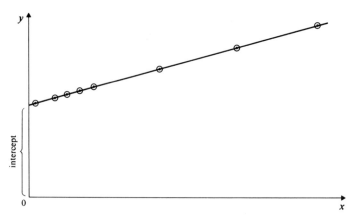

FIGURE 8   Extra points near the axis to measure an intercept.

(g) *Plot a graph as your experiment proceeds*   In this way you can check immediately if a point is so widely off that it needs repeating. You will also be able to check whether the points are reasonably evenly spaced, or whether you need some more closely spaced points (e.g. where the shape of the graph appears to be changing).

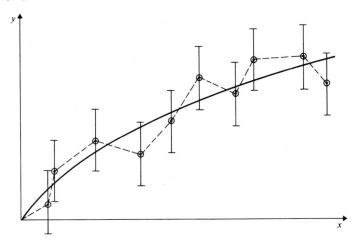

FIGURE 9   Two ways of drawing the 'best curve' through a set of points
Which of the two is correct depends on the circumstances.

(h)   *Draw a straight line or a smooth curve through points plotted on the graph*, rather than joining up successive points by short straight lines. In most cases, graphs represent some smooth variation of one quantity with another, and so a smooth curve is usually appropriate. Thus the continuous line in Figure 9 is usually preferable to the broken line.

SAQ 2   Table 3 shows the percentage of men surviving until various ages as ascertained in a particular survey. Draw and label axes on the graph paper in Figure

TABLE 3
Percentage of men surviving

Age/years	Percentage surviving
51	89.3
57	83.5
63	73.1
69	58.2
75	40.3
81	20.6

10, choose appropriate scales and ranges for the axes, and plot the results from Table 3 in graphical form (p. 38).

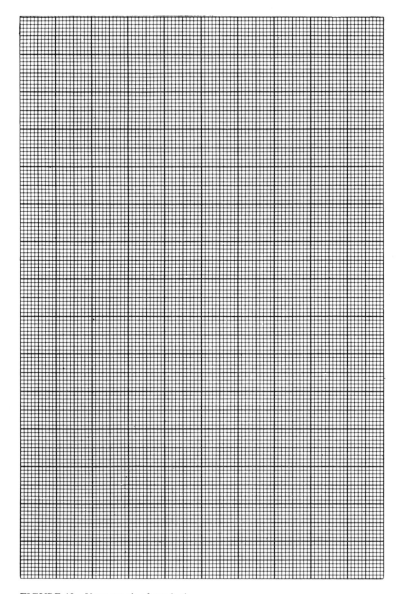

FIGURE 10   Your graph of survival.

SAQ 3   Having noted the speed of his car at various times (Table 4), a naive graph-plotter presents his measurements in the way shown in Figure 11. His graph can be criticized on at least five counts. Point out the shortcomings, and correct them by replotting the results in Table 4.

38

TABLE 4 Speed of car

Time/s	Speed/miles hr^{-1}
0	64
10	69
20	73
30	76
40	78
50	79

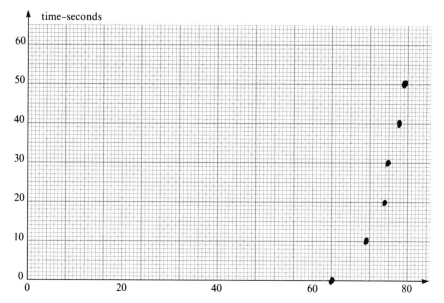

FIGURE 11   Naive plot of car speed.

3.3   Showing likely errors on graphs

In any quantitative scientific experiment, it is essential to indicate the likely
errors, or confidence limits, in any measured quantity. The most difficult part of
this procedure is actually assessing how large the error in a measurement could
be, and this problem was discussed in Section 2.2. However, once an error has
been estimated, it is straightforward to represent it on a graph. For example, if the
extensions measured in the wire stretching experiment (Table 1) are accurate to
± 0.05 mm, then the first two measurements would be represented graphically by

bars as shown in Figure 12. The *error bars* extend 0.05 above and below the measured points, which are indicated by the circled points. This representation implicitly assumes that the masses are known much more accurately, to ±0.2 kg or so, which is the radius of the circles. Suppose though that the masses were known only to the nearest kilogram, that is, to ±0.5 kg. This uncertainty would be represented by a horizontal error bar, which extends 0.5 kg on either side of the plotted mass as shown in Figure 13. Generally both horizontal and vertical error bars should be shown, and either of them omitted only if the associated error bar is too small to plot on the graph.

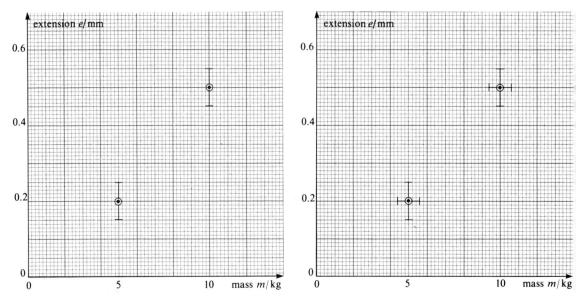

FIGURE 12   Vertical error bars indicate that the extension is known to ±0.05 mm. The absence of horizontal error bars implies that the mass is known much more accurately.

FIGURE 13   Vertical and horizontal error bars. The horizontal error bars indicate an error of ±0.5 kg.

Plotting error bars is slightly more complicated if you are not plotting a measured quantity x directly, but are plotting x^2, x^3, $\sin x$, etc.

We shall illustrate the procedure by taking as an example an experiment in which the speed v of a falling ball is measured after it has dropped through various distances s. Results of the experiment are tabulated in the first two columns of Table 5 and we shall assume that the possible error in the speeds is ±0.5 m s^{-1}, and the possible error in the distances is ±0.2 m.

TABLE 5   Data on a falling ball

A	B	C	D	E	F	G
distance	velocity	v^2	$s + \Delta s$	$s - \Delta s$	$(v + \Delta v)^2$	$(v - \Delta v)^2$
s/m	v/m s^{-1}	$(\mathrm{m\,s}^{-1})^2$	m	m	$(\mathrm{m\,s}^{-1})^2$	$(\mathrm{m\,s}^{-1})^2$
1.0	4.4	19.3	1.2	0.8	24.0	15.2
2.0	6.0	36.0	2.2	1.8	42.3	30.3
3.0	7.9	62.4	3.2	2.8	70.6	54.8
4.0	8.7	75.7	4.2	3.8	84.6	67.2
5.0	9.7	94.1	5.2	4.8	104.0	84.6
6.0	11.1	123.2	6.2	5.8	134.6	112.4

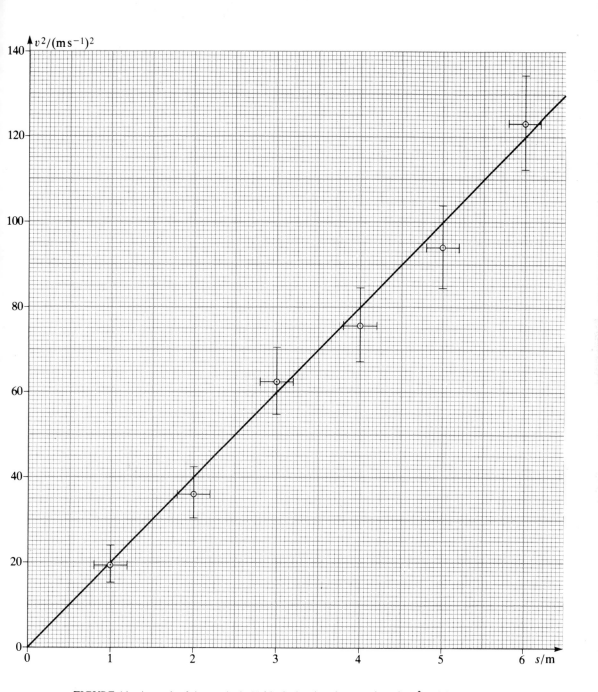

FIGURE 14   A graph of the results in Table 5, showing the error bars for v^2 and for s.

Suppose that we have already discovered, by plotting various graphs, that v^2 is proportional to s. Using the data in columns A and C of Table 5, we get the plot shown by the circled points in Figure 14. Working out the error bars on s is straightforward—we simply work out $s + \Delta s$ and $s - \Delta s$ (columns D and E in Table 5), plot both against v^2, and draw the error bar between them. To produce the error bars on v^2, we work out $(v + \Delta v)^2$ and $(v - \Delta v)^2$ (as shown in columns F and G of Table 5), plot them against s, and draw the error bar between them, as shown in Figure 14. The important point here is that if we estimate that there is a possible error of $\pm\Delta v$ in the measured value of v, then we mean that we are reasonably confident that the speed lies within the range $v-\Delta v$ to $v+\Delta v$. It therefore follows that the (speed)^2 should lie within the range $(v-\Delta v)^2$ to $(v+\Delta v)^2$, and so we use these values to determine the error bars. Note that even though the size of the errors in v are all the same, the errors in v^2 get larger as v gets larger.

The presence of error bars on a graph serves a number of useful purposes. If the graph is one which we would expect to be a smooth curve then we would expect the results to be scattered around that curve by amounts ranging up to the size of the error bar. Should the results deviate from a smooth curve by much more than the error bars, as shown in Figure 15, then either we have underestimated the errors, or the assumption that a smooth curve should describe the results is not valid. On the other hand, if all of the results deviate from the expected curve by much less than the error bars, as in Figure 16, then we might well have over-estimated the likely errors. An alternative explanation in this latter case would be that the dominant contribution to the error bar was from a systematic error that would shift all results in the same direction by as much as the error bar.

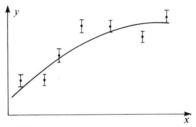

FIGURE 15   Have the error bars been underestimated?

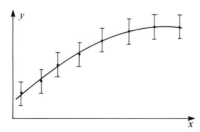

FIGURE 16   Have the error bars been overestimated?

Error bars are also very helpful in identifying mistakes in measurements or plotting of points. For example, Figure 17 shows measurements of the amount of heat needed to raise the temperature of 1 kg of a rare metal known as gadolinium by 1 °C at various temperatures. All results lie on the broken line except for one, which deviates from the straight line by about three times the magnitude of the error bar. This immediately suggests a mistake.

In cases like this, the plotting of the point on the graph should be checked first of all, and any calculations made to get the numbers plotted should be checked as well. If these don't show up a mistake, then the measurements that gave rise to the suspect point should be repeated. In some cases, of course, repeating the measurements is just not possible, and one is left with the difficult decision about whether

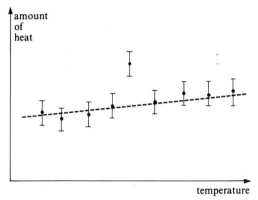

FIGURE 17 An apparently odd point when gadolinium is heated.

to ignore the point or not. No hard and fast rule can be made about this, but you should always be aware that what appears to be an anomalous measurement may indicate a real (and possibly as yet undiscovered) effect.

In the case of gadolinium, more detailed measurements show that the real behaviour is as shown by the continuous line in Figure 18. By ignoring the apparently anomalous result, we would have overlooked a real anomaly (which is, in fact, caused by the magnetic properties of gadolinium).

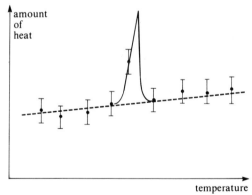

FIGURE 18 An anomaly in the specific heat of gadolinium, which could have been overlooked if one point was discarded.

An important piece of advice follows from this: if at all possible, plot a graph while you are taking measurements. If you do this, you can immediately check for errors and investigate any anomalies that appear. Plotting as you go along also helps to ensure that the results are reasonably distributed on the graph, and this usually means having them equally spaced.

43

3.4 Straight-line graphs: slopes and intercepts

The slope of a straight-line graph is given by:

$$\text{slope} = \text{rise/run}$$

and, using the graph in Figure 19, you can see in that case:

$$\text{slope} = \frac{\text{rise}}{\text{run}} = \frac{57\,\text{m}}{10\,\text{s}} = 5.7\,\text{m s}^{-1}$$

It is important to remember always to *include the units* when quoting the value of the slope. Remember also that the slope of the line is constant, and does not depend on which pair of points on the line are used to calculate it. However, we can only read off the coordinates of the points with limited accuracy, and so, in practice, different pairs of points will produce slightly different values of the slope. Note that the best practice is to choose two points that are as widely separated as possible, since then the errors in reading the coordinates will be a much smaller fraction of the difference between the coordinates than if the points were close together.

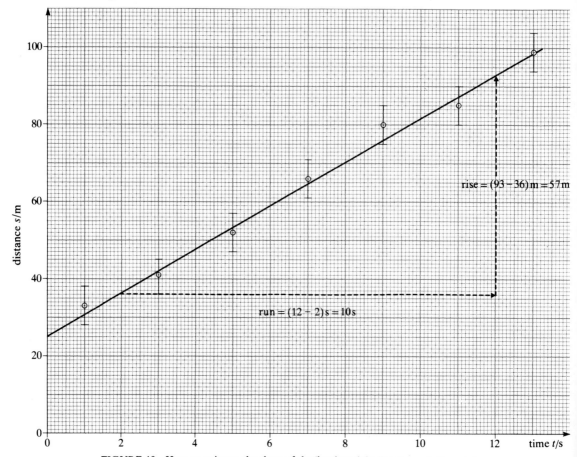

FIGURE 19   How to estimate the slope of the 'best' straight line through the points.

The straight line in Figure 19 is the one we think is best fitted to the results plotted. Displacements of some points above the line are balanced by displacements of other points below the line. However, the error bars indicate the uncertainty in the experimental results, and other lines with different slopes could be drawn to pass through all of the error bars. So in order to estimate the uncertainty in the slope, we draw lines that pass through all of the error bars with the maximum and minimum possible slopes. These lines are shown in Figure 20, and their slopes are $6.2 \, \text{m s}^{-1}$ and $4.9 \, \text{m s}^{-1}$ respectively. These values differ from the slope of the 'best' straight line by $0.5 \, \text{m s}^{-1}$ and $0.8 \, \text{m s}^{-1}$, an average difference of $0.7 \, \text{m s}^{-1}$. We therefore quote the value of the slope as $(5.7 \pm 0.7) \, \text{m s}^{-1}$.

The other quantity that is normally used to specify the position of a straight line on a graph is its intercept with the vertical axis. The equation of a straight line can always be written in the form:

$$y = mx + c$$

where m is the slope of the line and c is the intercept with the y-axis—that is, the value of y when $x = 0$ (as can be seen from the equation). This line is shown in

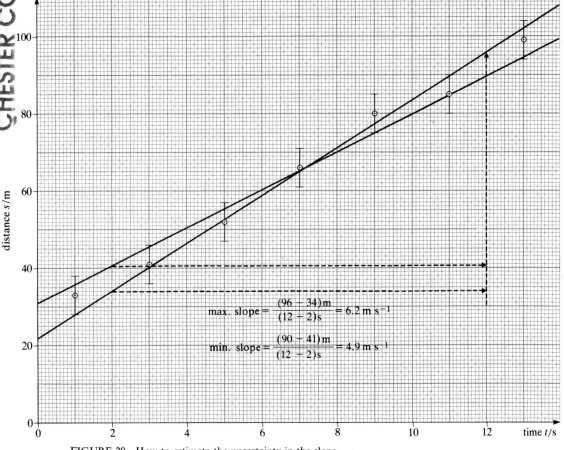

FIGURE 20 How to estimate the uncertainty in the slope.

Figure 21. In the case of the results shown in Figure 19, the intercept is at $y = 25$ m and, since this is determined from the 'best' straight line, we regard it as the best estimate of the intercept. Note that again we must quote the appropriate units for the intercept. The maximum and minimum likely values of the intercepts are found by drawing other lines through the error bars, and in this case they are the intercepts of the lines with maximum and minimum slopes shown in Figure 20. These intercepts are 31 m and 22 m respectively, and the mean difference between these and the best intercept is 5 m. We can, therefore, quote the experimentally determined intercept as (25 ± 5) m.

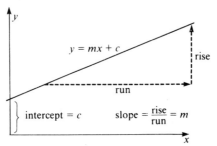

FIGURE 21   A graph of the straight line $y = mx + c$, showing how the slope and intercept are related to m and c.

Having now determined both slope and intercept *and* the possible errors in each, we can summarize the experimental results in Figure 19 very succinctly in the form of an equation, namely:

$$s = (5.7 \pm 0.7)\,\mathrm{m\,s}^{-1} \times t + (25 \pm 5)\,\mathrm{m}.$$

3.5   Converting curves to straight lines

In many cases, if you plot the dependence of one variable in an experiment against another, the sequence of experimental points will be curved in some way, and cannot be fitted by a straight line. In such cases, it is much more difficult to draw a line on the graph to represent the average behaviour, and even more difficult to deduce what equation might represent the results. However, it is often possible to plot such results in an alternative way so that a straight line *is* obtained, and an equation can then readily be deduced. Of course, the real problem then is deciding what to plot along each axis in order to get a straight line.

If we know *a priori* the form of the equation relating the measured quantities, then the decision is fairly easy. Take the example of the dependence of speed v of a ball against distance fallen s, that we discussed in another context in Section 3.3. If we had plotted v against s, we would have obtained the graph shown in Figure 22— certainly not a straight line. However, if you happen to know about motion due to gravity, you would be able to predict that $v^2 = ks$, where k is a constant. Now, since a straight line has an equation of the form $y = mx + c$, if we plot v^2 along the vertical axis and s along the horizontal axis the results will fall around a straight line as shown in Figure 14. Comparing the two equations:

$$y = mx + c \qquad v^2 = ks$$

v^2 corresponds to y; both are plotted vertically

s corresponds to x; both are plotted horizontally

k corresponds to m; both are the slope of the lines

the intercept on the v^2 axis is zero, and this corresponds to c.

Writing the equations together shows this correspondence clearly:

$$v^2 = ks + 0$$
$$\updownarrow \quad \updownarrow\updownarrow \quad \updownarrow$$
$$y = mx + c$$

Now we shall look at another (more complicated) example. It can be shown theoretically that the time t taken for an object to slide down a smooth plane inclined at an angle θ to the horizontal is given by the equation:

$$t^2 = \frac{n}{\sin \theta}$$

where n is a constant. (Don't worry about how this equation was derived.) If we compare this equation with the standard form of the straight-line equation:

$$t^2 = n \times \frac{1}{\sin \theta} + 0$$
$$\updownarrow \quad \updownarrow \quad \updownarrow \quad \updownarrow$$
$$y = m \quad x \quad + c$$

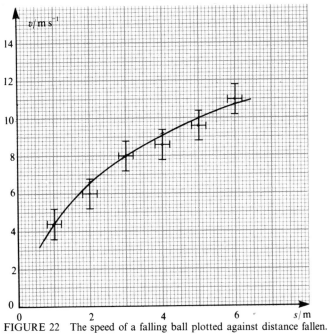

FIGURE 22   The speed of a falling ball plotted against distance fallen.

we can see that what we need to plot is t^2 against $(1/\sin\theta)$. If we do this, we expect a straight line with slope n and intercept at $t^2 = 0$.

So what advantages, or additional information, do we get by plotting graphs in such a way as to get a straight line? First, we can confirm (or disprove!) the predicted form for the behaviour. Looking at Figure 22, it is difficult to say whether v^2 is proportional to s: the graph is curved, as one would expect, but is it curved in precisely the way predicted by $v^2 \propto s$? By plotting v^2 against s, as in Figure 14, we can readily see whether a straight line is consistent with the experimental results and, since it is, we can conclude that the results are consistent with the prediction $v^2 \propto s$. Second, by determining the slope and intercept of the straight line, we can actually deduce numerical values of constants in the equation relating measured quantities. Thus, from the slopes of straight-line plots, we readily deduce values of k and n in the two examples given above. Getting these values from curves would be extremely difficult.

Another important advantage of a straight-line graph is that it is extremely easy to extrapolate beyond the range of measured values: you only need a ruler. Extrapolating a curve is far more difficult and is subject to much more uncertainty.

3.6 The use of logarithmic graph paper

Table 6 gives the data for the mortality of 200 moth eggs over a 12-month period. Numbers of adult moths surviving were counted on six occasions in the last five months of the study period.

TABLE 6   Number of moths surviving

Date	Number (N)
1/3/75	200*
1/9/75	16
15/9/75	13
1/10/75	11
1/11/75	7
15/1/76	2
1/2/76	2

* This is the number of eggs. All other numbers are of adult moths.

When this data is plotted, the graph shown in Figure 23 is obtained. This is not a very convenient way of plotting data. Six of the seven experimental points are clustered together near the bottom right-hand corner of the graph, leaving a large gap between 16 survivors and the original 200 eggs. The shape of the curve we have drawn is largely a matter of guesswork.

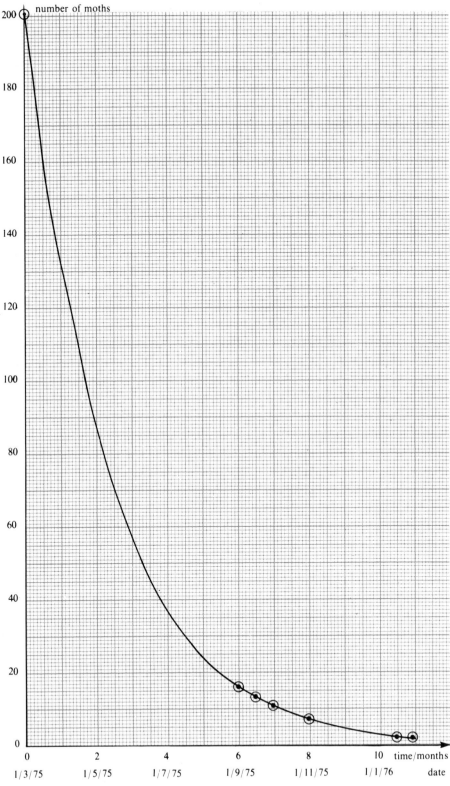

FIGURE 23   A graph showing the mortality of 200 moth eggs over a 12-month period.

Whenever you come across data like this, which range over a few orders of magnitude or where there are big gaps between the points, it is often more useful to plot the *logarithm** of the data. When you do this, you sometimes find that the result is a straight line. There are many logarithmic relationships in science. The data that we need to plot are in Table 7, and log N is plotted against time in Figure 24.

You can see from Figure 24 that we obtain a graph in which the points are more evenly spaced and we can more easily draw a line through the points. Admittedly, our line doesn't go through all the points, but this is hardly surprising when the difference of one moth makes such a large change in the position of a point on the right of our graph.

Working out the log values for such a plot is a trifle tedious (even with your calculator!) and of course it introduces another step between the data and the graph, which could introduce some additional error in the result.

The way around this is to use graph paper where the lines on one axis have been drawn in a logarithmic fashion. On the paper in Figure 25 the horizontal scale is an ordinary one, in which the large divisions are divided into tenths and each division has the same size. The vertical scale is however a *logarithmic* scale, in which each *power of ten or decade corresponds to the same length of scale.* Figure 25 shows the moth data plotted on this *semi-logarithmic paper.* (p. 53.).

Notice that, in each decade, the divisions become progressively compressed towards the upper end, in the same way as the logarithms of numbers increase more slowly than the numbers themselves. Table 8 compares the logarithmic scale and the linear scale.

TABLE 8   Comparison of logarithmic and linear scales

number N	log N	N on log scale	log N on linear scale
10	1.000	10	1.0 = log 10
		9	
9	0.954	8	0.9
		7	log 7
8	0.903	6	0.8
7	0.845	5	0.7
6	0.778	4	0.6
			0.5
5	0.699	3	log 3
			0.4
4	0.602	2	0.3
3	0.477		0.2
2	0.301		0.1
1	0	1	0 = log 1

*See Appendix 1, Logarithms, p. 83.

50

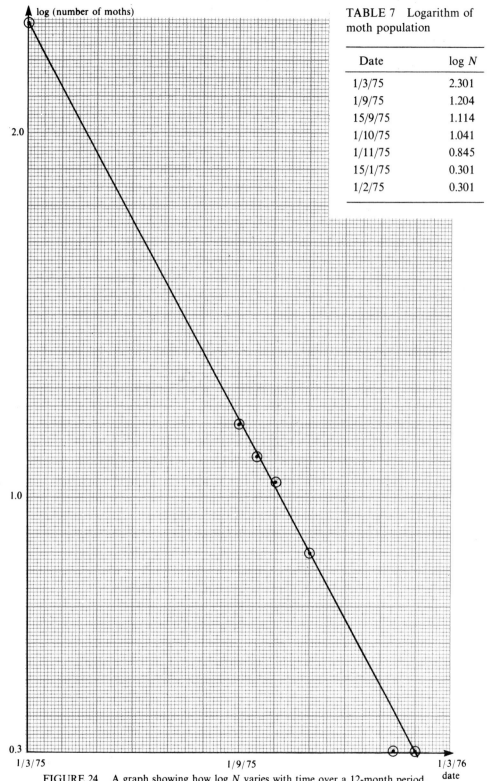

FIGURE 24   A graph showing how log N varies with time over a 12-month period.

As you can see, points plotted on logarithmic graph paper will be distributed in just the same way as the logarithms of the corresponding numbers would be distributed on ordinary graph paper. Figures 24 and 25 show this clearly.

What is the slope of the line in Figure 25? If we replace log N by y as the dependent variable, i.e. log $N = y$, and call time t we have a straight-line graph of y against t.

This graph has a constant slope (which we shall call k) and it has a y-intercept (which we shall call b). It may therefore be represented by this equation:

$$y = b + kt \qquad (13)$$

We can find the values of b and k from the graph

When $\qquad\qquad t = 0$, $N = 200$, so $y = \log N = 2.30$

so $\qquad\qquad y = 2.30 + kt$

When $\qquad\qquad t = 11$ months, $N = 2$, so $y = \log N = 0.30$

our equation is $\quad 0.30 = 2.30 + 11k$

The slope is $\qquad\qquad k = -\dfrac{2.0}{11}$

Notice that k is negative, because N (and log N) decreases as t increases.

So the equation of the straight line is:

$$y = \log N = 2.3 - \frac{2.0}{11} t \qquad (14)$$

How can we turn equation 14 (which tells us how the logarithm of N depends upon the time t) into an equation which tells us how N depends upon t?

To do this we need to recall the definition of a logarithm (see Appendix 1).

If $\qquad\qquad\qquad\qquad A = 10^x$

$$\log A = x$$

Equation 14 may be transformed slightly to put it in a form that will allow us to make use of the definition of log N. Let N_0 stand for the value of N at $t = 0$; in this example $N_0 = 200$ and log $N_0 = 2.3$. Now the slope of the graph is k; in this example $k = -2.0/11$.

Then equation 14 becomes:

$$\log N = \log N_0 + kt$$

or $\qquad\qquad \log N - \log N_0 = kt$

i.e. $\qquad\qquad \log \dfrac{N}{N_0} = kt \qquad (15)$

so $\qquad\qquad \dfrac{N}{N_0} = 10^{kt}$

or $\qquad\qquad N = N_0 \, 10^{kt}$

$$= 200 \times 10^{-(2.0/11)t}$$

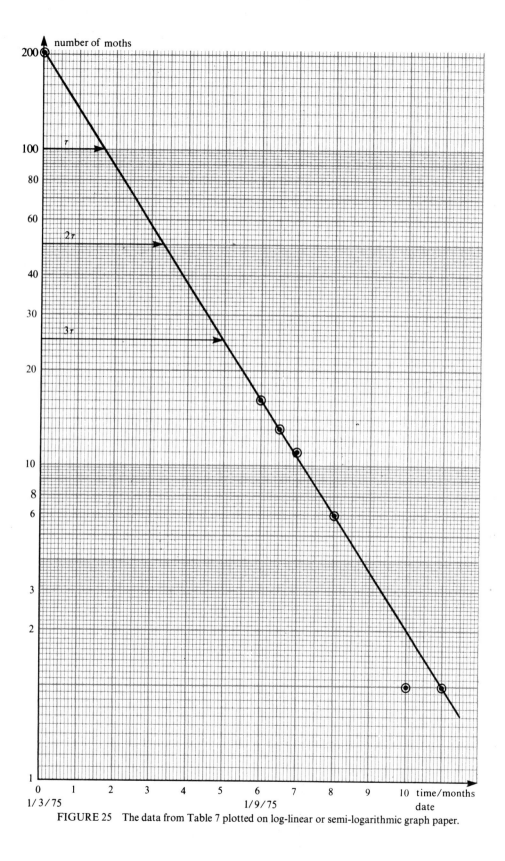

FIGURE 25   The data from Table 7 plotted on log-linear or semi-logarithmic graph paper.

This is the equation of the curve plotted in **Figure 23**. It shows a population that is decreasing in such a way as to be halved every 1.65 months. Thus, starting at 200, it drops to 100 at 1.65 months, to 50 at 3.3 months, to 25 at 5 months, to 12.5 at 6.6 months and so on. This population is said to be decreasing logarithmically, with a *half-life* of 1.65 months.

This mode of decrease, or 'decay', which is also called 'exponential decay', is characteristic of many natural phenomena, from populations subject to predation, to radioactive elements subject to instability.

The equation for exponential decay may be written in another form, in which the half-life appears explicitly. We have equation 15:

$$\log \frac{N}{N_0} = kt \tag{15}$$

If we call the half-life τ (the Greek letter 'tau', pronounced 'taw'), then:

when $t = \tau$ $\qquad\qquad N/N_0 = \frac{1}{2}$

i.e. $\qquad\qquad \log \frac{1}{2} = k\tau \quad$ or $\quad k = \frac{1}{\tau} \log \frac{1}{2} \tag{16}$

Substituting for k in equation 16:

$$\log \frac{N}{N_0} = \frac{t}{\tau} \log \frac{1}{2} = \log \left(\frac{1}{2}\right)^{t/\tau}$$

(If you did not understand this last step, refer again to Appendix 1.)

i.e. $\qquad\qquad \frac{N}{N_0} = \left(\frac{1}{2}\right)^{t/\tau} \tag{17}$

In the example we have been considering:

$$k = -\frac{2.0}{11}$$

i.e. from equation 16

$$\frac{1}{\tau} \log \frac{1}{2} = -\frac{2.0}{11}$$

$$\tau = -\frac{11}{2} \log \frac{1}{2} = -\frac{11}{2} (-0.301) \approx 1.65$$

As the above analysis shows, it is convenient to plot such processes on logarithmic graph paper, both because the logarithmic scale gives equal space to each order of magnitude and because the graph will be a straight line if the relationship is in fact logarithmic, or 'exponential'. Furthermore, as you can see from **Figure 25**, the half-life can be read simply and directly off the graph.

The type of graph paper illustrated in **Figure 25** is called log-linear or semi-logarithmic paper, because one axis is marked off on a logarithmic scale and the other on an ordinary linear scale. It is useful, as you have seen, for plotting a quantity that varies by several orders of magnitude against another quantity that does not. In the example we have just considered, N varies from 200 to 2, i.e. by two orders of magnitude, while t varies from 0 to 11, i.e. by one order of magnitude.

Sometimes we find that we wish to plot a graph where both variables range over several powers of ten. For example, consider the data in Table 9 which show how one quantity T depends on another quantity R.

TABLE 9   Variation of R with T

R	0.058	0.108	0.150	0.228	0.778	1.427	2.869	4.498	5.900
T	0.24	0.62	1.00	1.88	11.86	29.46	84.02	164.8	247.7

R varies by two orders of magnitude and T varies by three orders of magnitude. It would thus be convenient to plot *both* T and R on a logarithmic scale. For this you need 'log-log' graph paper. In Figure 26, we have plotted T against R on log-log graph paper (p. 56). The points lie upon a straight line.

To find the slope of a straight line plotted on log-log paper, you simply measure off a convenient baseline, such as the line AB, which we have made 8.3 cm long, and then measure the vertical line BC, which in this case is 12.5 cm long.

So the slope is $BC/AB = 12.5/8.3 = 1.5$.

This procedure is, of course, valid only if the logarithmic scales on both axes are the same, that is, each step in the powers of 10 has the same length on each axis. In such a case the slope is also the proportionality constant between log T and log R.

The equation of this straight line is thus:

$$\log T = \text{constant} + 1.5 \log R$$

It will be convenient to let the constant be $\log k$, so:

$$\log T = \log k + 1.5 \log R$$
$$= \log (kR^{1.5})$$

i.e.
$$T = kR^{1.5}$$

or
$$T^2 = KR^3 \text{ where } K = k^2$$

You may recognize this as a relationship between the period and the main radius of planetary orbits (Kepler's Third Law).

SAQ 4   Table 10 gives data for the mean growth in length (in mm) of a sample of moth caterpillars from the time they emerge from the egg to when they turn into a pupa. What type of graph (linear, log-linear or log-log) is most suitable to illustrate this data graphically.

TABLE 10   Growth of moth caterpillars

time days	mean length l mm
1	0.2
3	0.5
7	2.2
10	6.7
15	30.2

55

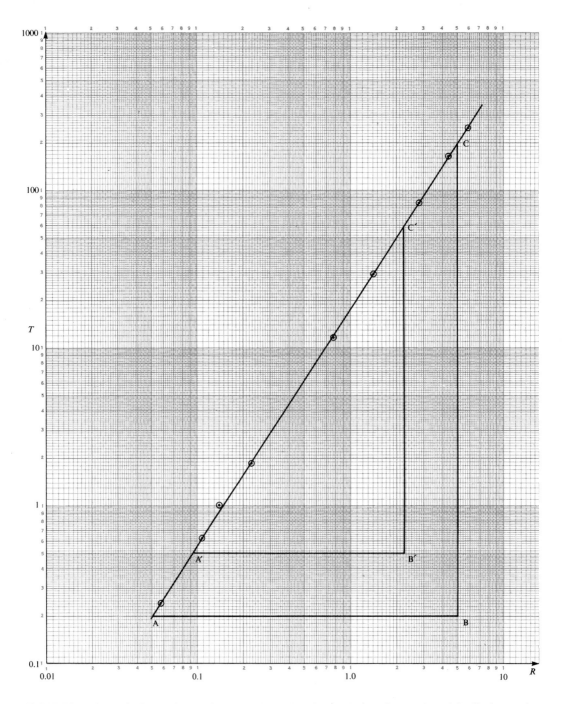

FIGURE 26   The graph of a quantity T against a quantity R, plotted on 'log-log' graph paper. As explained in the text, the relation between T and R is $T^2 = KR^3$. (Note that when finding the slope of a straight line, the use of a large triangle ABC is preferable to A′B′C′; given the same ruler, fractional errors are reduced.)

56

4 Distributions

In Section 2 we showed you how to take the mean value of a set of measurements of the volume of water flowing from a pipe, and how to estimate the likely error in the value. In this Section we introduce ways of expressing the range of values in a set of measurements and how the values are distributed about the mean value. The kind of expressions we introduce here are important in quoting data on populations encountered in Biology and Earth sciences, as well as in expressing the reliability of a value that is the average of several measurements.

4.1 Distribution of measurements

Suppose that a colleague wants to know the volume of water issuing from a tube in a given time. She has your data from the water-flow experiment in Section 2.2, i.e. the volume of water collected over a four-minute period on five occasions was 436.5 cm², 437.5 cm², 435.9 cm³, 436.2 cm³ and 436.9 cm² (average 436.6 cm³). She also has a value of her own: 436.0 cm³. She wants the best possible value. She cannot choose one and ignore the other, for she has no grounds for making such a choice. Does she take the mean of the two results:

i.e. $$\frac{436.6 + 436.0}{2} = 436.3 \, cm^3 \quad ?$$

If she had taken only one reading, viz 436.0 cm³, you would naturally feel upset that a single reading taken by somebody else should carry as much weight as the mean of your five readings.

If the single reading taken by the second experimenter had the same reliability as any one of the readings you took, what would be the best estimate in these circumstances?

$$\bar{x} = \frac{436.5 + 437.3 + 435.9 + 436.4 + 436.9 + 436.0}{6}$$

$$= 436.5 \, cm^3$$

Alternatively, of course, her value of 436.0 cm³ may have been the average of more readings than you took.

If the second experimenter had taken 20 readings of the same reliability as yours, what would be the best estimate?

There is no need to know what the 20 individual values were. If the average of 20 readings was 436.0, the sum of these 20 readings will be 20 × 436.0, whatever the individual readings were. And if the average of your 5 readings was 436.6, their sum will be 5 × 436.6, whatever the individual readings were. So the sum of all 25 readings is

$$(20 \times 436.0) + (5 \times 436.6) = 10\,903\,\text{cm}^3$$

and so $\bar{x} = 10\,903/25 \approx 436.1\,\text{cm}^3.$

Clearly the number of readings taken is one important factor in determining the precision of a result. Is it the only factor?

Take a look at Figure 27. In Figure 27a are displayed the five readings that gave a mean value of $436.6\,\text{cm}^3$. In Figure 27b are five other possible readings giving the value of $436.0\,\text{cm}^3$. If the number of readings were the sole criterion for judging the precision of a result, the two values—436.6 and $436.0\,\text{cm}^3$—would carry the same weight. Does it look from Figure 27 as though they ought to? It would seem not. The measurements in the second set agree with each other more closely. Perhaps the second experimenter had a better way than you had of cutting off the water flow at the end of the given time period. It is only right that she should be given credit for her extra care. *The extent to which the readings are spread about the mean position has to be taken into account.*

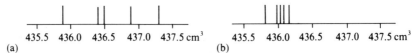

435.5	436.0	436.5	437.0	437.5 cm³

(a)   (b)

FIGURE 27   A set of five measurements of a volume: (a) with a wide spread; (b) with a narrow spread.

A rough and ready way of indicating this spread is to find the difference between the mean and the highest or lowest reading (whichever is further away from the mean) and take the spread to be about 2/3 of that difference.

In the example we have been considering, the mean of the first set of measurements was $436.6\,\text{cm}^3$ and the differences range from $+0.7$ to -0.7, as shown in the third column of Table 11. So in this case a rough estimate of the spread would be: spread $\approx 2/3 \times 0.7 \approx 0.5\,\text{cm}^3$

You will appreciate that if just one reading happened to be much further off the mean than all the others, this way of estimating the spread could be misleadingly pessimistic, and common sense would suggest that you should ignore that odd reading in making the estimate of spread.

The method is evidently subjective as well as rough and ready. If it is impossible to make more than one or two measurements of some quantity, this simple 'difference method' of estimating the error will obviously not work at all. We shall return to the question of what to do in such circumstances.

An objective method of reporting the spread in a set of measurements which has significance for statisticians is to calculate a quantity called the *standard deviation s*. If you quote the spread of your results in terms of the standard deviation, other people will know exactly what you mean. Furthermore, we know from statistical theory that, provided that s has been found from a large number of readings, about two-thirds of the readings will be within $\pm s$ of the true value of the quantity being measured. The method of calculating the standard deviation is illustrated in the bottom part of Table 11.

First calculate the mean. Then calculate the differences, by subtracting the mean from each individual reading. (We have called these differences d in Table 11.) Now calculate the square of each of these differences. (We have done this in the fourth column of the Table. Note that d^2 is always a *positive* quantity.) Now add up all the values of d^2 and divide this sum of the number of measurements (five in this example). Call this quantity s^2 ($s^2 = 0.224\,cm^6$ in this example). Now take the square root of s^2 to get s. ($s = 0.47\,cm^3$ in this example). We have rounded it off to

TABLE 11 Estimate of the standard deviation

Volume of water $\overline{cm^3}$	Mean value $\overline{cm^3}$	Differences d $\overline{cm^3}$	Square of differences d^2 $\overline{cm^6}$
436.5		−0.1	0.01
437.3		0.7	0.49
435.9	436.6	−0.7	0.49
436.4		−0.2	0.04
436.9		0.3	0.09

Sum of (differences)^2:	$1.12\,cm^6$
(Sum of (differences)^2)/5:	$s^2 = 0.224\,cm^6$
Standard deviation:	$s = 0.47\,cm^3 \approx 0.5\,cm^3$

$0.5\,cm^3$ because the individual readings differed from each other by a few tenths of a cm^3, so a value of $0.47\,cm^3$ is too precise.

The result of the experiment in this example would thus be stated as:

$$volume = (436.6 \pm 0.5)\,cm^3$$

In this case the 'rough-and-ready' estimate happened to be the same as the standard deviation. With more than just a few readings, the standard deviation would give a more reliable and less pessimistic measure of the spread than the rough-and-ready method would.

We can represent the procedure for calculating s, which we have just illustrated, by an algebraic formula, in which the individual readings are denoted by x_1, x_2, x_3, x_4, $x_5 \ldots x_n$ (there were only 5 readings in the previous example but, of course, there could have been any number), and the differences are represented by d_1, d_2, $d_3 \ldots d_n$.

Then, if $\bar{x}$ is the mean (average) value, the differences are simply:

$$d_1 = x_1 - \bar{x}$$
$$d_2 = x_2 - \bar{x}$$

and so on

$$d_n = x_n - \bar{x}$$

and the standard deviation is

$$s = \sqrt{\frac{d_1^2 + d_2^2 \cdots + d_n^2}{n}} \tag{18}$$

Note that the square root of a positive number may be either positive or negative.

For instance, $\sqrt{16} = +4$ or -4, since $(+4)\times(+4)=16$ and $(-4)\times(-4)=16$. Unless otherwise stated, it is understood throughout *HED* that we are taking the *positive* square root, i.e. that s is a *positive* number.

If s has been determined for a sample consisting of a great many readings, it gives a measure of how far individual readings are likely to be from the true value. It can be shown from statistical theory that about 68 per cent of the readings will lie within $\pm s$ of the true value, 95 per cent within $\pm 2s$, and 99.7 per cent within $\pm 3s$.

If there are many readings of the same quantity, it is difficult to make a quick assessment of the precision of an experiment and the likely mean value by examining a long list of numbers displayed in a table. It is more convenient to plot the readings in the form of a *histogram* (Figure 28).

The range of measured values is divided into equal intervals and a note made of the number of readings falling within each interval. For instance, as illustrated in Figure 28, the intervals may be from zero up to, but not including 1 s; from 1 s up to, but not including, 2 s; from 2 s up to, but not including, 3 s; and so on.

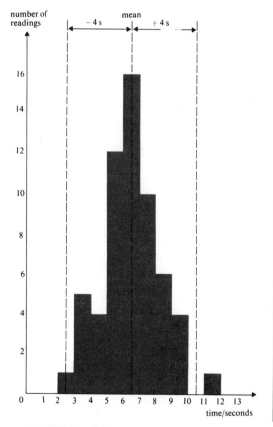

time interval/ seconds	number of readings in each interval
0–1	0
1–2	0
2–3	1
3–4	5
4–5	4
5–6	12
6–7	16
7–8	10
8–9	6
9–10	4
10–11	0
11–12	1
12–13	0

FIGURE 28   A histogram.

The number of readings in each interval determines the height of the histogram for that interval. For instance, in the histogram shown in Figure 28, the number of readings between 6 and 7 seconds is 16. With this histogram you can see at a glance that the mean value is about 6.5 seconds and the spread is about ± 4 seconds. Using the 'rough-and-ready' rule, you might quote the result as (6.5 ± 2.7) seconds. The standard deviation calculated from the data in Figure 28 works out at ± 1.8 seconds. As expected, the rough estimate is on the pessimistic side. It gives too much weight to the highest and lowest readings.

As the number of readings is increased, so one can take smaller and smaller intervals and still have a reasonable number of readings in each. Eventually, the 'step-like' character of the histogram is no longer noticeable and one is left with a smooth curve as in Figure 29. Strictly speaking, it is only when there are very large numbers of readings that one can say: 68 per cent of the readings will be within $\pm s$ of the true value, and 95 per cent within $\pm 2s$.

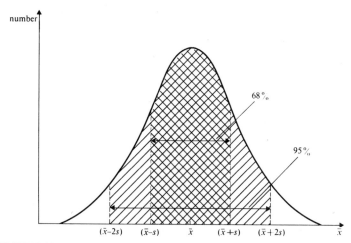

FIGURE 29   Distribution of a large number of readings about a mean value.

So much for the question of how far an individual reading is likely to be from the true value. This, however, is not our main concern, because normally you will take several readings and find the mean. We are more interested in how far the mean of the reading $\bar{x}$ is from the true value. Of course, it is not possible to say exactly how far away an individual reading is from the true value. We must emphasize that *we have no way of telling what the true value is*. However, it is desirable to be able to assign a probability to the mean lying within a certain range of the true value.

This range will depend not only on the spread of the individual readings but also on n, the number of such readings. It is, in fact, specified by a quantity called the *standard error on the mean* s_m, and is estimated through the equation

$$s_m = \frac{s}{\sqrt{n-1}} \qquad (19)$$

It is such that the mean value of a given sample (e.g. $\bar{x}$) has a 68 per cent chance of lying within $\pm s_m$ of the true value, 95 per cent within $\pm 2s_m$, etc. Therefore, s_m is a measure of how close the mean value of the given sample $\bar{x}$ is to the unknown true value. Once again we must stress that, unless you are prepared to take a course in statistics, this is an equation you must simply accept and use as a tool. But note the difference between the standard error on the mean s_m and the standard deviation of the individual measurements s.

In the experiment we have been considering, $\bar{x}$ is the mean of the five readings and has a value of $436.6 \, \text{cm}^3$. Now calculate the standard error on it, using the value we have already calculated for s, i.e. $0.5 \, \text{cm}^3$.

For this problem, n in equation 19 has the value 5, and s is 0.5

$$s_m = \frac{0.5}{\sqrt{5-1}} = \frac{0.5}{2}$$

$$= 0.25 \approx 0.3 \, \text{cm}^3$$

$$\bar{x} = (436.6 \pm 0.3) \, \text{cm}^3$$

Note that the units, in this case cubic centimetres, apply both to the mean value and its error. Therefore we have included both these numbers in the brackets.

Let us reiterate that, just because one assigns a standard error s_m to a result (for example, $\pm 0.3 \, \text{cm}^3$ on a mean value of $436.6 \, \text{cm}^3$), it does not follow that the true value necessarily lies within the specific range (i.e. within the range 436.3 to $436.9 \, \text{cm}^3$) as would be the case if we were specifying an engineering tolerance. *It is a convention*—one that is understood by all scientists to mean that there is a 68 per cent *chance* of the true value lying in that range, and that there is a 95 per cent chance of the true value lying within $\pm 2s_m$ of the mean value.

Note that the two statements—(i) the true value has a 68 per cent chance of lying within $\pm s_m$ of the mean value and (ii) the mean value has a 68 per cent chance of lying within $\pm s_m$ of the true value—are equivalent.

One important use of the standard error on the mean is in deciding about the significance of an experimental result. Suppose that a new theory suggests that a particular physical quantity should have the value 100 units. An experiment is done in which a large number of measurements are made of this quantity. The mean value is found to be 90 units and the standard error on the mean ± 11 units.

Does this experiment confirm the theory, or refute it?

The expected value (100) lies within $\pm s_m$ of the experimental mean (90 ± 11), but only just. Thus the probability that the experiment confirms the theory is certainly no higher than 68 per cent. Indeed, one could argue that since the expected value lies close to the edge of the experimental interval (79–101), there is only just over 32 per cent chance that the theory is supported by the experiment

Suppose, instead, that the result had been (90 ± 4) units. In this case, the 'true value', assuming it is 100 units, differs from the mean by more than twice the standard error. It follows that the chances that the theory is *wrong* are greater than 95 per cent.

Note from equation 19 that as the number of readings in the sample n increases, the quantity $\sqrt{n-1}$ increases and s_m gets smaller. However, it does so only slowly because $(n-1)$ appears as a square root. Thus a tenfold increase in the number of readings improves the precision by a factor of 3. A large number of sloppy readings, therefore, is no substitute for taking care and keeping the spread of the individual readings, and hence s, as small as possible.

If we combine equations 18 and 19 by substituting for s in equation 19 the value given by equation 18, we have:

$$s_m = \frac{s}{\sqrt{n-1}} = \sqrt{\frac{d_1^2 + d_2^2 + \cdots + d_n^2}{n(n-1)}}$$

and if n is large, so that $n - 1 \approx n$ and hence $n(n-1) \approx n^2$,

$$s_m = \frac{1}{n}\sqrt{(d_1^2 + d_2^2 + \cdots + d_n^2)} \tag{20}$$

If you are using a calculator to calculate s_m, it is an easy matter to add up all the values of d^2 in the memory, then take the square root and divide by n.

You should now be able to calculate the mean value, the standard deviation and the standard error on the mean value of a set of measurements subject to random error, using one or other of the formulae which we have collected together for your convenience in Table 12.

TABLE 12   Calculation of random errors

Mean value $\bar{x} = (x_1 + x_2 + \cdots + x_n)/n$ $\quad\quad\quad n = $ number of measurements of x	(21)

'Rough-and-ready' estimate of spread:

$$s \approx \frac{2}{3} d_m$$

where d_m is the maximum difference, up or down, between $\bar{x}$ and any of the values of x.

Standard deviation $s = \sqrt{\dfrac{d_1^2 + d_2^2 + \cdots + d_n^2}{n}}$	(22)

where $d_1 = x_1 - \bar{x}$, $d_2 = x_2 - \bar{x}$, ... $d_n = x_n - \bar{x}$.

Standard error on the mean $s_m = \dfrac{s}{\sqrt{n-1}}$	(23)

To a good approximation, if n is large compared with 1,

$$s_m = \frac{1}{n}\sqrt{d_1^2 + d_2^2 + \cdots d_n^2} \tag{24}$$

To test your understanding of the calculation of random errors try the following SAQs.

SAQ 5 The body masses of twenty male marmoset monkeys were obtained as part of a study on the growth of marmosets.

The masses in grams (g) of the 20 individuals at 600 days after birth were as follows: 280, 275, 283, 264, 272, 280, 290, 287, 283, 276, 278, 282, 280, 288, 282, 265, 291, 282, 283, 278.

(a) Make a rough estimate of the spread of masses about the mean.

(b) Calculate the standard deviation.

(c) Calculate the standard error on the mean.

SAQ 6 An experiment was carried out to measure the period of oscillation of a pendulum. The mean value of a hundred measurements was 12.701 seconds, with $s_m = \pm 0.047$ seconds.

The theoretically predicted period of oscillation is 12.604 seconds. If the theory is correct, what is the chance of obtaining the above value in a properly conducted experiment? What could such a result indicate?

4.2 Skewed distributions

Of course, the perfectly symmetrical distribution of observations about a mean value, shown in Figure 29, is idealized and is rarely achieved in nature. It is more usual to find that the mean value is not the most 'popular' value in the distribution. For example, if you were to stand on a motorway bridge and make a survey of the lengths of the cars passing beneath you, then you would be very likely to obtain a distribution like that in Figure 30, because the most popular cars are of less than

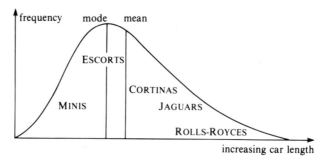

increasing car length

FIGURE 30   A positively skewed distribution of car lengths on a motorway.

average (mean) length. There is also a larger range of sizes among the large cars on the motorway, and this gives the distribution a 'tail'. By definition, Figure 30 shows a positively skewed distribution. On the other hand, if you were to include all the vehicles on the motorway in your survey at a time when the number of lorries exceeded the number of cars, then the range of car sizes would form the 'tail' and the distribution might be *negatively* skewed (Figure 31).

How can we make a quantitative measure of skewness? We know from Figure 29 that 68 per cent of the values in a symmetrical frequency distribution lie within one standard deviation of the mean. In all examples, we shall assume that 50 per cent of the observations lie to either side of the mean value ($\bar{x}$ is defined strictly as the sum of the x values of all the observations divided by the number of observations—equation 21—and is close to the 50 per cent mark of most distributions). The two points that have values of x at $\pm s$ from the mean in a symmetrical

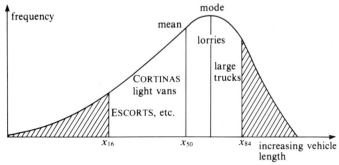

FIGURE 31 A negatively skewed distribution of all vehicle lengths on a motorway at a time when the number of lorries exceeds the number of cars. The 16, 50 and 84 percentiles have been marked, and each of the shaded areas includes 16 per cent of the observations.

distribution will occur, therefore, at the points $(50 + 68/2) = 84$ and $(50 - 68/2) = 16$. So, in Figure 29, 16 per cent of the observations lies to the left of the point $(\bar{x} - s)$ and 84 per cent lie to the left of the point $(\bar{x} + s)$. In the symmetrical distribution, these 16 and 84 *percentiles*, as they are known, are equidistant from the mean (or 50 percentile). But in a skewed distribution this is no longer the case. *By plotting a graph of the results* of our observations we can read off the x values at 16, 50 and 84 per cent points in our distribution. This gives a numerical value for skewness as follows:

$$\text{skewness} = \frac{(x_{84} - x_{50}) + (x_{16} - x_{50})}{2}$$

$$= \frac{(x_{84} + x_{16}) - 2(x_{50})}{2}$$

If you look at this equation, you will see that if there is a 'tail' of smaller vehicles (Figure 31), then the value of $(x_{50} - x_{16})$ will be more than $(x_{84} - x_{50})$. Now $(x_{16} - x_{50})$ must always be a negative number, and so the skewness will be *negative* (negative skewness) and vice versa for Figure 30. In Figure 29, skewness is zero and this defines the symmetrical distribution.

The importance of skewed distributions is demonstrated in the interpretation of grain sizes in different samples of sand. Although accumulations of sand on beaches, on sand dunes and in the bed of a river may appear to be all the same, we find that the ranges of grain sizes present vary tremendously depending upon whether the sand was blown by the wind, carried by water in a river or winnowed gently by waves. The populations of sand grains are often positively or negatively skewed and geologists can use this property of skewness to help them decide how an *ancient* sand deposit, now formed into a solid rock, was originally laid down.

5 Reporting data

Many of the early scientists took little care to report their findings. It was as though they considered the results of their experiments a private matter; fodder for their own curiosity. However, with the development of technology capable of exploiting new scientific discoveries, this attitude changed. It became clear that scientists who did not publicize their findings could needlessly delay the pace of technological advance, and possibly forfeit the credit for their discoveries, losing not only fame, but possible material rewards as well.

For example, an eighteenth-century British scientist, Henry Cavendish, came, through his experiments, to a deep understanding of electrical phenomena. He had, however, one serious fault—he rarely took the trouble to write up his findings. The result was that for many years people continued working on problems he had solved long ago. For example, he discovered Ohm's law of electrical resistance fifty years before Ohm did. Yet the law is quite rightly ascribed to Ohm, because it was the German schoolmaster who made the information available to others. Moral: you may get personal satisfaction from doing good experimental work but, if you wish to get credit for it and to benefit the community at large, you have to develop an ability to communicate your findings to others.

Such an ability is particularly important when results challenge orthodox thinking. The chemical world had to wait 50 years for the insight into chemical bonding which derived from the work of Avogadro in the early nineteenth century. His work was ignored during his lifetime, but brilliantly publicized by his countryman Cannizaro at one of the first scientific conferences, a gathering of chemists at Karlsruhe in 1860. It is noteworthy that it was not verbal argument which convinced most of the chemists present, but the distribution of a pamphlet in which Avogadro's results and arguments were set out clearly and forcibly. So, skill in the presentation of experimental results and conclusions derived from them is something that is in the interests of every scientist to acquire. It does not matter how skilful your experimental technique is or how careful your observations are, if you fail to communicate clearly both the results and their significance to your reader, this skill and care will have been pointless.

5.1 Writing reports

It is important to distinguish between the style in which you keep your laboratory notebook (which is your personal diary) and that in which you write up your final report.

The main requirement of the notebook is that it should contain all necessary information in a form that is accessible to *you*. The final report must still contain all necessary information, but organized in a form accessible to the average reader, and retrievable in as short a time as possible. Clarity, conciseness, and presentation are all at a premium; any conclusions you reach should be stated simply, with a clear indication of their limitations. There are a few basic rules for the presentation of experimental reports, which you should find useful.

1 The first component of your report should be an *abstract*, which summarizes the work in a very few sentences. (It may not be the first thing that *you* write, but nonetheless it should appear at the beginning because it helps your reader 'see the wood for the trees' while working through the necessarily detailed treatment of experimental results.)

2 The abstract should be followed by a short couple of sentences that explain the principles of your approach (basically, *how you set about obtaining your data*) and any special precautions or techniques that you used.

3 Your experimental data are the focal point of your report. It is worth taking some trouble *to organize data into an easily digestible form*. Where possible (even if the data are qualitative) use a table. Allow plenty of space for this so that the results are not cramped.

4 Often a graph can be used to summarize the relationship between two quantities. Graphs should always be supported by appropriately labelled tables of raw data. It is important to remember to *include all the original data* in your report; it is impossible for someone else to judge your work if the data are incomplete. (You could find it difficult enough yourself to make sense of an incomplete report in a couple of months time!) Careful recording of data will prevent the need to repeat the experiment to supply missing data.

5 All *tables, graphs and drawings should be labelled* as, for example, 'Table A', 'Figure 2' and referred to where necessary in your account by that label. When drawing diagrams (or graphs) you should initially use a pencil rather than a pen so as to be able to make corrections if necessary. The drawings should be made large; do not think that by using a thick pencil and cramming the drawing into a small space you can avoid being careful over details.

6 Discussion of the results should *include any assumptions and approximations made*, and comments on the limitations of the apparatus, extending for quantitative work to an assignment of error limits on the result quoted. It is a good idea to make suggestions at this stage about how experimental design could be improved by reducing the dominant error, and about how the phenomenon being studied could be investigated more thoroughly and extensively. Make sure to include a discussion of any unexpected behaviour, and a comparison of your result with the predictions of theory, if this is appropriate.

7 Any arguments you make in *discussion* should be capable of being followed by someone without much background in the subject. It is better to use simple terms which you fully understand than more complex jargon which you may misuse. Throughout the discussion try to *cut down on unnecessary words and information*. Although in presenting data you can hardly be too generous with information, the ideal to aim for in presenting arguments is a concise style, avoiding irrelevancies and repetition. It is a good plan to reread your report critically after a lapse of a few hours or even a day to make sure that it is easy to read, and that it says exactly what you mean to say. The changes that you will almost certainly want to make at this stage are bound to be improvements!

8   Lastly, you should present, in summary form, the *conclusion* of your experiment. It may take the form of a verbal generalization, or it may be a numerical result, which should never be separated from the estimate of its error limits. If you are studying the transformations involved in a chemical reaction, you should express your conclusions in the form of a chemical equation; if you are studying the relationship between measured quantities, (such as, for example, distance and time) you should include an equation relating the quantities under study.

9   Finally, let us stress that your account should be *a full and faithful record* of what you have done. If, for example, during the experiment, you took certain precautions and made certain checks, but subsequently omitted to point these out in your account, it will be assumed that you did not do them and, moreover, that it did not even occur to you that you ought to have done them.

5.2   Summary: a 40-point check list

For easy reference, we summarize below the most important points relating to data handling and reporting. Keep referring to them until, with experience, they become second nature to you.

Planning an experiment

1   If possible perform a quick preliminary experiment as a rehearsal, in order to allow you to plan the way you will do the experiment.

Keeping a laboratory notebook

2   Do not use scraps of paper; put readings and comments into a special note-book kept for the purpose.

3   Record all readings directly; do not rely on the accuracy of your mental arithmetic.

4   Record readings in tables with columns headed with the name and unit, in such a way as to make the numbers in the columns dimensionless.

5   Underline important quantities (for example, mean values).

6   Do not overwrite numbers, cross out the wrong number and record the new one alongside.

7   Record all your observations.

8   Write notes on all you do.

9   Use plenty of space.

Hints on calculations

10   Average raw readings rather than processed data in order to save the labour of unnecessary multiplications.

11   Check calculations by carrying out the operations in reverse order.

12   Check the order of magnitude of your result (by using rounded off numbers).

13   Ask yourself whether the result of a calculation or measurement looks reasonable.

14   Use powers of 10 to avoid the impression that noughts used for placing the decimal point are significant figures.

15   Suppress meaningless digits arising from calculations. The final result of a multiplication or division can have no more significant figures than those possessed by the factor with the fewest.

16   In suppressing meaningless digits, avoid rounding-off too crudely. Check that inaccuracies introduced by rounding-off are negligible compared with the experimental error.

Errors

17   Always estimate errors in experimental measurements and calculated results.

18   Where independent measurements are combined to find the value of a quantity, use the appropriate formula for combining errors. These are listed for easy reference on p. 27.

19   Only quote errors to one (or maybe two) significant figures.

20   Any error smaller than about a third of the dominant error can be ignored.

21   Special care is needed when two almost equal quantities have to be subtracted, or when a measured quantity is to be raised to a power.

22   Find out early in an experiment what the dominant errors are and (if necessary) concentrate your time and effort on reducing these.

Hints on how to plot graphs

23   Plot the dependent variable (i.e. the one that changes as a result of alterations you make to the other) along the vertical axis, and the independent one along the horizontal axis.

24   Label the axes with the name of the quantity and the unit, in such a way as to make the quantities plotted dimensionless numbers.

25   Choose scales so that the points are widely spread over the page.

26   Use a simple scale.

27   Plot points as small dots in circles or crosses.

28   Include error bars, or error crosses if there are errors in both variables.

29   In general, put a smooth curve through the points, not a zig-zag.

30   Spread readings evenly over the range unless an intercept on an axis is to be measured (in which case have several readings close to the axis concerned).

31   Plot the graph as the experiment proceeds.

32   Whenever possible choose your variables so as to get a straight line. This applies to variables related by an expression of the form $y = mx + c$.

Writing reports

33 Preface your report with a short abstract.

34 Do not repeat obvious details and theoretical derivations that may be given as a background in the laboratory manual; just refer to them.

35 Mention all precautions and checks—you cannot get credit for them otherwise.

36 Discuss assumptions, approximations, consistency of readings, random and systematic errors, limitations of apparatus, suggestions for improvements, abnormal behaviour, comparison of result with that expected, etc.

37 Draw well-labelled diagrams of apparatus. Drawings of specimens should be done initially at least in pencil, and should be large. Where necessary, you should indicate the scale.

38 Refer in the text to all tables and figures.

39 Every physical quantity calculated should have a unit, the correct number of significant figures, and an estimated error.

40 End your report with a brief summary of the conclusions you have reached from the experiment.

If you follow the advice contained in this summary, and apply it in your practical work, you should acquire an ability not only to present data, but also to detect errors or deficiencies in somebody else's presentation. You may like to check your ability to do this by trying SAQ 7.

> **SAQ 7**   Read the following account of an experiment in which the extension of an elastic rubber band is measured as a function of its load. Imagine you are a tutor assessing the work. Criticize the design of the experiment and comment on the adequacy of reporting. To which deficiencies of presentation would you draw most attention?
>
> *Report*
> A set of accurately calibrated weights was obtained; these were known to be accurate to $\pm$ 0.001 g. The rubber band was attached by means of a hook to a fixed point (the underside of a cupboard) and a mark made on it by means of a felt pen. Each weight was tied in turn to the end of the rubber band, using a light but strong thread, and the position of the mark for each load measured with a ruler. The Figure shows the apparatus. The results are as listed in the table.

Mass/g	Position of mark
0	3.9
200	6.7
300	7.9
1 700	17.5
1 800	17.7

Conclusion

The effect of applying force to the rubber band is to cause it to elongate. An extension of 13.8 is produced by a loading of 1 800. The reason that this extension is possible is that the band is made of a polymer which can exist both in a coiled and an uncoiled form. In the coiled form, weak interactions between polar side chains hold the coils together; however, these weak interactions are easily overcome, allowing the coils to straighten out under the extending force.

6 Units

6.1 Basic SI units

The system of units now generally adopted is known as SI. This is an abbreviation for Système Internationale d'Unités. It was formally approved in 1960 by the General Conference of Weights and Measures.

In the SI system there are seven basic units (Table 13).

TABLE 13

Physical quantity	Name of unit	Symbol for unit
length	metre	m
mass	kilogram	kg
time	second	s
electric current	ampere	A
thermodynamic temperature	kelvin	K
luminous intensity	candela	cd
amount of substance	mole	mol

Symbols for units do not take a plural form (e.g. 5 kilograms is written 5 kg not 5 kgs).

6.2 Supplementary SI units

In addition to the seven basic units there are two supplementary units associated with angular measurements:

Physical quantity	Name of unit	Symbol for unit
plane angle	radian	rad
solid angle	steradian	sr

6.3 Derived SI units

The units shown in Table 14 are derived from the basic units, but for convenience they are assigned special names.

6.4 Units to be allowed in conjunction with SI

Certain units have proved so popular among scientists that, although strictly speaking there is no further need for such units, they are nevertheless being retained and are shown in Table 15. Notice that these are now defined in terms of SI units although originally they were not.

TABLE 14

Physical quantity	Name of derived unit	Symbol for derived unit	Symbol as expressed in SI units
energy	joule	J	$kg\,m^2\,s^{-2}$
force	newton	N	$kg\,m\,s^{-2} = J\,m^{-1}$
power	watt	W	$kg\,m^2\,s^{-3} = J\,s^{-1}$
electric charge	coulomb	C	$A\,s$
electric potential difference	volt	V	$kg\,m^2\,s^{-3}\,A^{-1} = J\,A^{-1}\,s^{-1}$
electric resistance	ohm	Ω	$kg\,m^2\,s^{-3}\,A^{-2} = V\,A^{-1}$
electric capacitance	farad	F	$A^2\,s^4\,kg^{-1}\,m^{-2} = A\,s\,V^{-1}$
magnetic flux	weber	Wb	$kg\,m^2\,s^{-2}\,A^{-1} = V\,s$
inductance	henry	H	$kg\,m^2\,s^{-2}\,A^{-2} = V\,s\,A^{-1}$
magnetic induction	tesla	T	$kg\,s^{-2}\,A^{-1} = V\,s\,m^{-2}$
luminous flux	lumen	lm	$cd\,sr$
illumination	lux	lx	$cd\,sr\,m^{-2} = lm\,m^{-2}$
frequency	hertz	Hz	s^{-1}
customary temperature, θ_C	degree Celsius	°C	$\theta_C/°C = T/K - 273.15$
pressure	pascal	Pa	$Pa = N\,m$

TABLE 15

Physical quantity	Name of unit	Symbol for unit	Definition of unit
length	parsec	pc	$30.87 \times 10^{15}\,m$
area	barn	b	$10^{-28}\,m^2$
	hectare	ha	$10^4\,m^2$
volume	litre	l	$10^{-3}\,m^3$
pressure	bar	bar	$10^5\,N\,m^{-2}$
mass	tonne	t	$10^3\,kg = 1\,Mg$
kinematic viscosity, diffusion coefficient	stokes	St	$10^{-4}\,m^2\,s^{-1}$
dynamic viscosity	poise	P	$10^{-1}\,kg\,m^{-1}\,s^{-1}$
magnetic induction	gauss	G	$10^{-4}\,T$
radioactivity	curie	Ci	$37 \times 10^9\,s^{-1}$
energy	electron-volt	eV	$\approx 1.6021 \times 10^{-19}\,J$

The common units of time (e.g. minute, hour, year) will persist, and also the angular degree.

6.5   Fractions and multiples of units

In some contexts, our units may be too large or too small. We can, of course, always get over the problem of writing many zeros before or after the decimal point by using powers of 10, for example, 10^{-6} kg instead of 0.000 001 kg. It is convenient, however, to have fractional or multiple units, and these are denoted by placing a prefix before the symbol of the unit.

It is normal to restrict the multiples and fractions of a unit to powers of 1 000 (hence the centimetre, which is 10^{-2} m, is not strictly in accord with SI). The allowed prefixes are shown in Table 16.

TABLE 16

Fraction	Prefix	Symbol	Multiple	Prefix	Symbol
10^{-1}	deci	d	10	deka	da
10^{-2}	centi	c	10^2	hecto	h
10^{-3}	milli	m	10^3	kilo	k
10^{-6}	micro	μ	10^6	mega	M
10^{-9}	nano	n	10^9	giga	G
10^{-12}	pico	p	10^{12}	tera	T
10^{-15}	femto	f			
10^{-18}	atto	a			

Compound prefixes should not be used, e.g. 10^{-9} metre is represented by 1 nm not 1 mμm.

Also note that until such time as a new name may be adopted for the kilogram (the basic unit of mass) the gram will often be used, both as an elementary unit (to avoid the absurdity of mkg) and in association with numerical prefixes, e.g. μg.

6.6   Other units

Finally, we append in Table 17 an assorted list of common units that run contrary to SI, together with their SI equivalent. The values are given in scientific notation to five significant figures. (In scientific notation, the quantity is expressed with *one* figure before the decimal point and with the appropriate power-of-ten multiplier.)

To test your facility with units and their fractions and multiples, you should try SAQs 8 and 9 preferably without referring back to the lists in this Section.

TABLE 17

Physical quantity	Unit	Equivalent
length	inch	2.5400×10^{-2} m
	foot	3.0480×10^{-1} m
	yard	9.1440×10^{-1} m
	mile	1.6093 km
	nautical mile	1.8532 km
area	square inch	6.4516×10^{-4} m^2
	square foot	9.2903×10^{-2} m^2
	square yard	8.3613×10^{-1} m^2
	square mile	2.5900 km^2
volume	cubic inch	1.6387×10^{-5} m^3
	cubic foot	2.8317×10^{-2} m^3
	U.K. gallon	4.5461×10^{-3} m^3
mass	pound (avoirdupois)	4.5359×10^{-1} kg
density	pound/cubic inch	2.7680×10^{4} kg m^{-3}
	pound/cubic foot	1.6019×10 kg m^{-3}
force	dyne	10^{-5} N
pressure	atmosphere	1.0133×10^{5} N m^{-2}
	torr	1.3332×10^{2} N m^{-2}
energy	erg	10^{-7} J
	calorie (thermochemical)	4.1840 J
power	horse power	7.4570×10^{2} W
temperature	degree Fahrenheit	$T/°F = (9/5)t/°C + 32$

SAQ 8 Match the list of physical quantities A–P below with the list of units 1–16:

A acceleration   B angle   C density   D electric charge   E length   F momentum   G frequency   H mass   I electric current   J volume   K amount of substance   L force   M time   N energy   O stress   P power

1 mole   2 newton   3 joule   4 kilogram per cubic metre   5 second   6 radian   7 metre per square second   8 watt   9 cubic metre   10 coulomb   11 kilogram   12 ampere   13 hertz   14 kilogram metre per second   15 newton per square metre   16 metre

75

SAQ 9 In Table 18 column A lists a fraction or multiple of a unit, column B lists another fraction or multiple of a unit, and column C gives the ratio of the quantities in column A to those in column B. Thus, for instance, $1\,km/1\,m = 10^3$ (row 1). Fill in the blank in each row of the Table.

TABLE 18

Row No.	A Unit A	B Unit B	C Ratio of Unit A/Unit B
1	1 km	1 m	10^3
2	1 µV	1 V	
3	1 mJ	1 MJ	
4	1 µA		10^{-6}
5		1 nm	10^6
6	1 ms	1 µs	
7		1 Hz	10^6
8		1 kW	10^{-3}
9	1 nm	1 cm	
10	1 µW	1 GW	
11	1 kV	1 MV	
12	1 dg	1 kg	
13		1 nC	10^{18}
14	1 mm^3	1 m^3	
15	1 µm		10^3
16		1 kN	10^{-6}
17	1 GJ		10^3
18		1 dm	10^4
19	1 ns	1 s	
20	1 kg	1 µg	

7 Dimensions

7.1 Derived SI units

In Section 6.3 we listed a number of *derived* SI units with special names. For example, the unit of frequency, the hertz, was defined as:

$$1\,\text{Hz} = 1\,\text{s}^{-1}$$

In the same list, you will find the unit of force, the newton, defined as:

$$1\,\text{N} = 1\,\text{kg}\,\text{m}\,\text{s}^{-2}$$

Why is $1\,\text{N} = 1\,\text{kg}\,\text{mg}^{-2}$?

Force = mass × acceleration (Newton's second law).

So if a mass of 1 kg is accelerated by $1\,\text{m}\,\text{s}^{-2}$ we have, by definition, a force of 1 N, i.e. $1\,\text{N} = 1\,\text{kg}\,\text{m}\,\text{s}^{-2}$.

7.2 Derived SI units, unit symbols and dimensions

A simpler example of a derived unit, which was not listed in Section 6.3 because it has no special name, is that of area, the square metre, written $1\,\text{m}^2$.

By way of an exercise, see if you can write the SI symbols for the quantities named and defined in Table 19.

TABLE 19

Physical quantity	SI unit and definition	Symbol for SI unit	Dimensions
area	square metre	m^2	
velocity	metre per second	$\text{m}\,\text{s}^{-1}$	
momentum	kilogram metre per second	$\text{kg}\,\text{m}\,\text{s}^{-1}$	
force	kilogram metre per second per second (newton)	$\text{kg}\,\text{m}\,\text{s}^{-2}$	
volume	cubic metre		
density	kilogram per cubic metre		
acceleration	metre per second squared (rate of increase of velocity)		
stress	newton per square metre (force per unit area)		
energy	newton metre (joule) (force times distance)		

The *dimensions* of a physical quantity indicate explicitly how that quantity is related to the seven basic quantities of Table 13. Area, for example, obtained by multiplying a *length* by another *length*, has the *dimensions of length squared*. In symbols:

$$[\text{area}] = [L^2], \text{ where } [L] = [\text{length}]$$

We use the *square brackets* to indicate that we are referring to the *dimensions* of the quantity inside the brackets. No matter what units the area is expressed in (e.g. square nanometres, square miles, or acres) its dimensions are always those of length squared, i.e. $[L^2]$.

> **SAQ 10**   In the expression for calculating the area of a triangle:
>
> $$\text{area} = \tfrac{1}{2} \text{ base} \times \text{ perpendicular height}$$
>
> what are the dimensions of the right-hand side?

A speed, which is obtained by dividing a distance by a time, has the dimensions of distance per time or distance × time^{-1}:

i.e. $$\text{speed} = [LT^{-1}], \text{ where } [T] = \text{time}$$

This is true whatever units are used, $m\,s^{-1}$ or m.p.h. or any other units. Similarly, the magnitude of momentum (mass × speed) and the magnitude of acceleration (speed/time) have the dimensions of $[MLT^{-1}]$ and $[LT^{-2}]$ respectively.

As a simple exercise, enter the appropriate dimensions in the fourth column of Table 19. Compare your list with the one in Table 20 at the end of Section 7.

Note that some quantities have units but are dimensionless. For example, angles are measured in units of degrees or in units of radians. In both cases, these units are defined as a ratio of one length to another. So the 'dimensions' of an angle are those of $[L/L] = 1$, i.e. an angle is dimensionless.

7.3   The use of dimensions to check formulae

One use of dimensions is as a check on whether you are using the right formula for something.

A valid physical equation applies both in respect of number *and of units* for each term. The consequence of this is that a change from one system of units to another does not invalidate the equation. For example, the statement:

$$\text{acceleration} = \text{velocity/time}$$

holds true irrespective of whether the magnitude of velocity is measured in miles per hour or millimetres per second.

Furthermore, *each term in a correct physical equation must have the same dimensions*. An equation which is not 'balanced' in terms of dimensions is certain to be wrong.

To take an example, you might decide that an expression of the form:

$$w_f = w_a - \rho \, \frac{g_E}{V}$$

describes how the weight of a body alters when it is in a fluid, where:

w_a is the weight in air (the force of gravity on the body),

w_f the apparent weight registered by the force on the balance when the body is immersed in fluid,

ρ is the density of the fluid,

g_E the acceleration due to gravity, and

V the volume of the body.

You should check whether your logic in deciding on this expression was correct, by examining its dimensional balance. The dimensions of the term on the left-hand side of the expression are simply those of force; i.e. $[MLT^{-2}]$, as is the first term on the right-hand side.

The second term on the right-hand side has the dimensions of density × acceleration ÷ volume:

i.e. $$[ML^{-3}] \times [LT^{-2}] \div [L^3] = [ML^{-5}T^{-2}]$$

This analysis shows at once that the original expression was wrong; further, it indicates the nature of the error. The discrepancy involves dimensions of length, which are much too small in the second term. The inference is that the volume terms should have appeared in the numerator rather than the denominator, and an expression of the form:

$$w_f = w_a - \rho g_E V$$

should be tried.

The dimensions of the second term on the right-hand side of this equation are:

$$[ML^{-3}] \times [LT^{-2}] \times [L^3] = [MLT^{-2}]$$

This equation *is* dimensionally balanced and, therefore, *may* be correct.

To take a somewhat more complex example, suppose you want to calculate the speed of propagation of a seismic wave through a part of the Earth's interior. You believe that the speed should depend on the ratio of the elastic modulus to the density, but you are not sure whether it is just proportional to this ratio, or to its square or square root, or to some other power of it.

The elastic modulus is the ratio of a stress to a strain:

$$modulus = stress/strain$$

The stress is a force per unit area, and the strain is a ratio of two lengths.

Thus

$$[modulus] = [force/area]/[length/length]$$

$$= [mass \times acceleration/area]$$

$$= [M \times LT^{-2}/L^2] = [ML^{-1}T^{-2}]$$

$$[density] = [mass/volume]$$

79

$$= [ML^{-3}]$$

$$\frac{[\text{modulus}]}{[\text{density}]} = \frac{[ML^{-1}T^{-2}]}{[ML^{-3}]}$$

$$= [L^2 \quad T^{-2}]$$

This ratio has the same dimensions as speed squared $[LT^{-1}]^2$. The dimensional analysis thus indicates that

$$\text{speed} \propto (\text{modulus/density})^{1/2}$$

but it does not tell us anything about the constant of proportionality.

TABLE 20

Physical quantity	SI unit and definition	Symbol for SI unit	Dimensions
area	square metre	m^2	$[L^2]$
velocity	metre per second	$m\,s^{-1}$	$[LT^{-1}]$
momentum	kilogram metre per second	$kg\,m\,s^{-1}$	$[MLT^{-1}]$
force	kilogram metre per second per second (newton)	$kg\,m\,s^{-2}$	$[MLT^{-2}]$
volume	cubic metre	m^3	$[L^3]$
density	kilogram per cubic metre	$kg\,m^{-3}$	$[ML^{-3}]$
acceleration	metre per second squared (rate of increase of velocity)	$m\,s^{-2}$	$LT^{-2}]$
stress	newton per square metre (force per unit area)	$N\,m^{-2}$	$[ML^{-1}T^{-2}]$
energy	newton metre (joule) (force times distance)	$N\,m$	$[ML^2T^{-2}]$

List of Objectives

Handling Experimental Data (*HED*) is not meant to be studied like a textbook. It is meant to be used for reference, particularly in conjunction with experimental work.

If you use *HED* in this way, it should help you to acquire certain skills and abilities. In particular, you should be able to do the following:

1   Given the results of a measurement in the form of a set of values of some measured quantity:

 (i)   calculate the mean value;

 (ii)   estimate by a 'rough-and-ready' method the deviation, or 'spread', about the mean value;

(iii)   calculate the standard deviation and hence calculate the standard error on the mean from the formula $s_m = s/\sqrt{n-1}$

(iv)   decide on the significance of an experimental result by comparing the mean value with the predicted value (given the relevant information about the probabilities that the true value lies within $\pm s_m, \pm 2s_m, \pm 3s_m$, etc., of the mean value—SAQs 5 and 6.

2   Given the relevant information about an experiment:

 (i)   make reasonable estimates of the probable errors;

 (ii)   decide which are likely to be the dominant errors;

(iii)   distinguish between systematic and random errors;

(iv)   when errors in two or more quantities are of comparable magnitude, combine them correctly to obtain an estimate of the resultant error, for sums and differences, products and ratios and for powers of the quantities concerned.

3   Given a presentation of the results of an experiment in the form of tables and/or graphs, identify errors or deficiencies of presentation in respect of: the recording of data in tabular form; the treatment of errors; the choice of variables, axes and scales of graphs; the manner in which the axes are labelled, the points plotted and the appropriate curve(s) drawn through the points on a graph.

(SAQs 2, 3 and 7)

4   (a) Specify the SI units for the following physical quantities:

length, mass, time, electric current, amount of substance, angle, frequency, force, acceleration, momentum, energy, power, stress, volume, density, electric charge, electric potential difference.

(b) Relate the following fractions and multiples to each other (illustrated here with reference to the unit of length):

$$nm \quad \mu m \quad mm \quad cm \quad dm \quad m \quad km \quad Mm \quad Gm$$

(SAQs 8 and 9)

5 (a) Express the dimensions of the quantities listed in Objective 4(a);

(b) Use dimensions to check the validity of formulae involving any of the quantities listed in Objective 4(a). (SAQ 10)

6 Report an experiment correctly using:

(a) tabulated data

(b) graphical presentation of data

(c) a concise description

(d) a summary

(e) estimates of errors

(f) a dimensional check of results

(SAQs 1 and 4)

Appendix 1   Logarithms

Logarithms are closely related to powers of numbers. Take for instance, the number 100. You can express this as a power of 10, thus:

$$100 = 10^2$$

Reading the same equation from right to left,

i.e. as $$10^2 = 100$$

you could say 'if ten is raised to the power two, that makes a hundred'.

If you ask: 'by what power must ten be raised to produce a hundred', what should the answer be? Clearly, the answer is 2.

Another way of saying the same thing is that the *logarithm* (to the base 10) of 100 is equal to 2,

$$100 = 10^2$$

$$\log_{10}100 = 2$$

You can have logarithms to any base. For example,

$$8 = 2^3 \qquad\qquad 81 = 3^4$$

$$\log_2 8 = 3 \qquad\qquad \log_3 81 = 4$$

The word 'logarithm' means 'a reckoning number', the name indicating the purpose for which logarithms were used when they were invented in the seventeenth century. The idea was that much tedious arithmetic could be avoided if multiplication and division could be replaced by addition and subtraction. This is made possible when all numbers are expressed in a form a^x, because, whenever a number $k(=a^x)$ is multiplied by a number j $(=a^y)$, then the product $k \times j$ is obtained by adding the indices x and y.

$$k \times j = a^x \times a^y = a^{x+y} = m$$

The logarithmic tables which were drawn up nearly four centuries ago, allow any number to be converted to its logarithm, and many generations of mathematicians and school children have been grateful for the simplification of their calculations which these tables permit. However, the advent of cheap electronic calculators has made the tables redundant as a computational aid, so you will not be using logarithms for this purpose. They are still used in science, however, to express the values of quantities that can vary over a wide range, so you should be familiar with their evaluation and manipulation.

The most commonly used logarithms are those to the base 10, and these are usually represented simply by log, i.e. the subscript $_{10}$, indicating that the base is 10, is usually omitted.

Exercise 1

(a) Use your calculator to find the logarithm to the base ten of: 1 000 10^6 10^9.

Do you agree with the answers it gives?

(b) Now use the calculator to evaluate to three figures: $\log_{10}3$ $\log_{10}6$ $\log_{10}9$ $\log_{10}300$.

(c) Use the calculator to find, to four figures, the numbers whose logs are: 4   0.3   1.3   3.3.

Before you do this try to make an estimate of the range (i.e. 1–10, 10–100, 100–1 000, 1 000–10 000) in which the number lies.

The definition of a logarithm (to the base 10) may be expressed more generally. If you choose any number k—which may be positive, negative, integral, fractional or zero—the number y defined by:

$$y = 10^k \text{ is } always \text{ positive.}$$

For example,
$$k = 1 \qquad y = 10^1 = 10$$
$$k = -1 \qquad y = 10^{-1} = 0.1$$
$$k = 0.5 \qquad y = 10^{0.5} = 10^{1/2} = \sqrt{10} \approx 3.16$$
$$k = 0 \qquad y = 10^0 = 1$$

The logarithm of y is defined as:

$$\log y = k \qquad \text{where } y = 10^k \tag{1}$$

Since y is always positive, there is no such thing as the logarithm of a negative number, i.e. *a negative number cannot be expessed in the form 10^k and hence have a logarithm (k).* But since log $y = k$ by definition, and k can be positive, negative, fractional or zero, so can log y be.

Exercise 2

(a) Without using your calculator, obtain a value for y when: log $y = -1$; 2; -2; 0.

Check your result using the calculator

(b) Now use your calculator to find the value of y, to 4 figures, when:

   (i)   log $y = -3.5$

   (ii) log $y = 0.5$

   (iii) log $y = 0.333\,3$

What other way can y be expressed for (ii) and (iii)?

Now suppose you have a product of two numbers $x = 10^m$ and $y = 10^n$. Then, remembering from the definition of logarithms that $m = \log x$ and $n = \log y$, and, applying the rules of indices:

$$xy = 10^m \times 10^n$$
$$= 10^{(m+n)}$$
so
$$\log(xy) = m + n$$
$$= \log x + \log y \qquad (2)$$

Similarly
$$x/y = 10^m/10^n$$
$$= 10^{(m-n)}$$
so
$$\log(x/y) = m - n$$
$$= \log x - \log y \qquad (3)$$

And if
$$x = 10^m$$
$$x^n = (10^m)^n$$
$$= 10^{mn}$$
So
$$\log(x^n) = mn$$
$$= n \log x \qquad (4)$$

To get used to the simple rules for manipulating logarithms, which we have shown you in equations 2–4, and to get practice in using your calculator to calculate the logarithms of numbers and the numbers with given logarithms, try the following:

1            $\log 1\,000 = 3$

2            $\log 10 \quad = 1$

3            $\log 2 \quad\;\; = 0.301\,03$

4            $\log 20 \quad = 1.301\,03$

5            $\log 200 \;\; = 2.301\,03$

Notice that $\log 20 = \log(10 \times 2) = \log 10 + \log 2$ (equation 2, above)
$$= 1 + 0.3010$$
and similarly $\qquad\qquad \log 200 = \log(100 \times 2) = 2.3010$

6   $\log 0.2$
$$\log 0.2 = \log (2 \times 10^{-1})$$
$$= \log 2 + \log 10^{-1}$$
$$= 0.301\,03 - 1$$
$$= -0.698\,97$$

7   $\log (2 \times 2)$
Well, in practice you
would first calculate:
2 × 2 = 4 and then find log 4. $\log 4 = 0.602\,06$
Check that log 4 = 2 × log 2. $0.301\,03 + 0.301\,03 = 0.602\,06$

8   $\log (3^{27})$
You could do this, too,
by first calculating
3^{27}, and then calculating the $3^{27} = 7.6256 \times 10^{12}$
logarithm of that number. $\log (7.6256 \times 10^{12}) = 12.882\,274$

Or you could calculate log 3 and then multiply it by 27 (equation 4).

Now try the following exercises:

Exercise 3

Use your calculator to complete the following Tables:

TABLE A   (give logs to three decimal places)

x	0.0031	0.089	0.560	1.270	9.863
$\log_{10} x$					

TABLE B   (give x to three figures)

$\log_{10} x$	7.25	3.18	1.02	0.94	0.02	-1.35
x						

Exercise 4

Very small numbers are sometimes handled in a logarithmic form of this type:

$$x = -(\log n)$$

Find n to three figures where $x = 10.25,\ 7.92,\ 3.00$.

Answers to Exercises in Appendix 1

Exercise 1 (a) 3, 6, 9. These follow from the definition of a logarithm: because

$$1\,000 = 10^3$$

$$\log_{10} 1\,000 = 3$$

The only room for error in using your calculator in this question is in entering the numbers 10^6 and 10^9.

(b) .477   .778   .954   2.48. Numbers between 1 and 10 have logs between 0 and 1, as you should expect. As 300 lies between 100 and 1 000 (i.e. between 10^2 and 10^3), its log is between 2 and 3.

(c) 10 000   1.995   19.95   1 995. 10^4 is 10 000, so it is easy to evaluate this without a calculator. This is not possible, however, when the logs are not integral, although you can see that the number whose log is 0.3 lies between 1 and 10, that whose log is 1.3 lies between 10 and 100 and that whose log is 3.3 lies between 1 000 and 10 000. Moreover, because of the properties of indices the number whose log is 1.3 is 10 times larger than the number whose log is .3, and the number whose log is 3.3 is 1 000 times larger.

Exercise 2 (a) Remembering that if $y = 10^k$:

$$\log y = k$$

we can see that $y = 10^{-1}$ or 0.1; 10^2 or 100; 10^{-2} or 0.01; and 10^0 or 1 respectively.

(b) (i) .000 316 2   (ii) 3.162   (iii) 2.154
In (ii), $y = 10^{1/2}$, which can also be written as $\sqrt{10}$.
In (iii), $y = 10^{1/3}$ or $\sqrt[3]{10}$.

Exercise 3 Using a calculator we can complete Table A and Table B as shown:

TABLE A

x	0.003 1	0.089	0.560	1.270	9.863
$\log_{10} x$	−2.509	−1.051	−0.252	0.104	0.994

TABLE B

$\log_{10} x$	7.25	3.18	1.02	0.94	0.02	−1.35
x	1.78×10^7	1.51×10^3	1.05×10^1	8.71	1.05	4.46×10^{-2}

Exercise 4 If $x = -\log n$, then $\log n = -x$, so n is the antilog of $-x$. Hence, n can be evaluated as 5.62×10^{-11}, 1.20×10^{-8} and 1.0×10^{-3} respectively.

SAQ answers and comments

SAQ 1 Provided a crude rounding-off is avoided, the limits of accuracy of d are determined by the accuracy of measurement of the angle, which was quoted as 0.1°:

$$\sin \theta = 0.709\,6 \text{ for the measured angle } 45.2°$$

$$= 0.710\,8 \text{ for the upper limit } 45.3°$$

$$= 0.708\,3 \text{ for the lower limit } 45.1°$$

Using $d = 1.667 \times 10^{-6}$ m the corresponding values for d are 591.5 mm for the measured angle, 592.5 mm and 590.4 mm respectively for the upper and lower limits of accuracy.

SAQ 2 The graph is shown in Figure 32. Notice how the axes are chosen—the independent variable is age. Notice too that the axes are labelled so that the numbers written on them are dimensionless. The choice of scale makes best use of the paper available. The points are plotted as dots within circles and they are joined by a smooth curve.

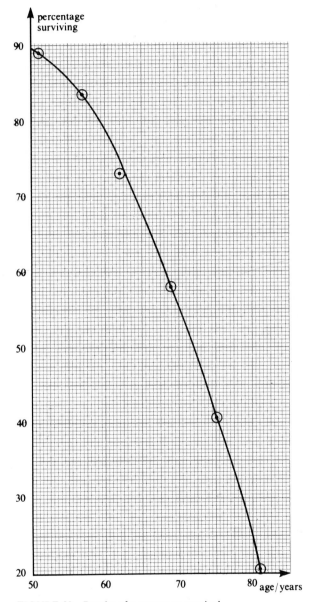

FIGURE 32   Results of a survey on survival.

SAQ 3 The faults with Figure 11 are:

1 the axes are chosen wrongly—the independent variable is time and it should be plotted on the horizontal axis;

2 the horizontal axis has no label;

3 the vertical axis should have the label time/seconds;

4 the choice of scale is poor on the horizontal axis;

5 the points should be small (or crosses), not large;

The correct plot of the data is shown in Figure 33.

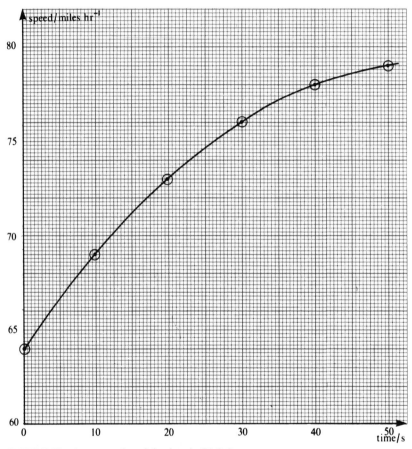

FIGURE 33 A correct plot of the data in SAQ 3.

SAQ 4 Since the mean length varies by more than two orders of magnitude, a logarithmic plot is most suitable to illustrate the data. If you tried to plot the data on linear graph paper, you would find (as Figure 34 shows) that the points are grouped at the bottom of the graph and that the plot is curved. The most suitable plot is a log-linear one with the mean length plotted on the log scale, as in Figure 35. Notice that this Figure uses three-cycle semi-log log paper because l varies by more than two orders of magnitude.

90

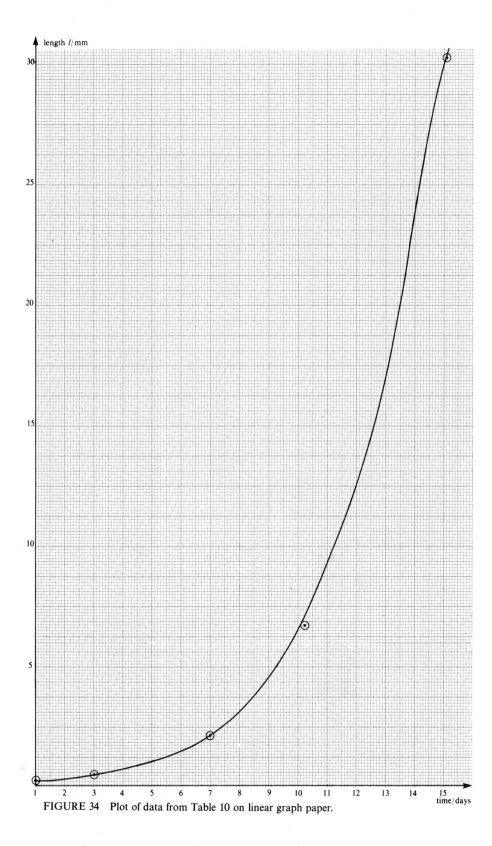

FIGURE 34   Plot of data from Table 10 on linear graph paper.

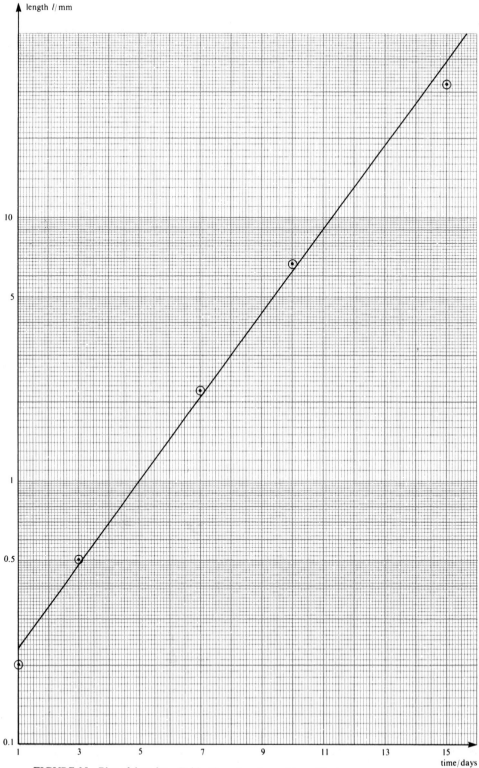

FIGURE 35   Plot of data from Table 12 on 3-cycle semi-logarithmic paper.

SAQ 5 (a) Using equation 21, the mean value is 280 g. The largest reading is 291 g which is 11 g above the mean, and the lowest reading is 264 which is 16 g below the mean.

Thus the spread $s \approx 2/3 \times 16\,g \approx 11\,g$ and the result could be quoted as mass $= (280 \pm 11)\,g$.

(b) We need to determine the values of $d = x - \bar{x}$ as shown in Table C, using $\bar{x} = 280\,g$

Using equation 22:

$$s = \sqrt{\frac{967\,g^2}{20}} = 6.95\,g \approx 7\,g$$

c) Using equation 23:

$$s_m = \frac{7\,g}{\sqrt{19}} \approx 1.6\,g$$

TABLE C

x/g	d/g	d^2/g^2
280	0	0
275	−5	25
283	+3	9
264	−16	256
272	−8	64
280	0	0
290	+10	100
287	+7	49
283	+3	9
276	−4	16
278	−2	4
282	+2	4
280	0	0
288	+8	64
282	+2	4
265	−15	225
291	+11	121
282	+2	4
283	+3	9
278	−2	4
Totals 5 599	(−1)	967

According to the previously explained meanings of s and s_m, note that approximately

68 per cent of x values from Table C lie within $(280 \pm 7)g$

95 per cent of x values from Table C lie within $(280 \pm 14)g$

Provided that our *sample* of 20 individuals was truly representative of the *whole population* of male marmoset monkeys, then the average mass for the whole population would be

with 68 per cent probability within (280.0 ± 1.6)g

with 95 per cent probability within (280.0 ± 3.2)g

SAQ 6 The theory (which is known to be correct) predicts that the period of oscillation should be 12.604 seconds.

The measured mean value of 12.701 seconds thus differs by just over $2s_m$ from the predicted value:

There is thus a less than 5 per cent chance that a mean value of 12.701 seconds could be found experimentally. The disagreement indicates a 95 per cent probability of some systematic error in the measurements.

SAQ 7 *Experimental design* Such accurately calibrated weights are not required; the tactic of tying them on to the rubber band with unspecified lengths of thread in any case destroys their calibration. (This increases all weights by an unspecified quantity.)

Marking with a felt pen is not a good idea, because the mark will be thick and imprecise to start with and will elongate as the rubber stretches, so it would be difficult to choose a reproducible place to read it.

The position on the band where the mark was made is not reported anywhere. One infers that it was *not* made at the bottom, in which case the extension of only part of the band has been studied.

The extension readings have been made in two groups; one at relatively low loading, one at high loading (close, in fact, to breaking point). Because the relationship at high loading is no longer linear, we have no firm information on behaviour at intermediate loading. Readings should have been spread evenly over the loading range studied.

Reporting and presentation An important omission, already noted, is failure to make clear the position of the felt pen mark on the rubber band. Nor have we been told or shown exactly how the ruler was placed to take readings of the mark, or more importantly, which units of length were used.

The Figure (which should have been labelled Figure 1) is uninformative on these important questions.

There should have been one or more additional figures. (Figure 2, etc.) displaying graphically the way in which extension depends on load.

The Table (which should have been labelled and referred to as Table 1) does not specify the units of length that were used.

94

The report does not start with an abstract, and the conclusion merely states (without units) the result of one reading. There is no general statement about how extension depends on load, and no indication of error limits on the result quoted.

The final sentences may or may not be true, but as they are not based on the results of this experiment, they should not appear in a conclusion.

SAQ 8

A	acceleration	7	metre per square second
B	angle	6	radian
C	density	4	kilogram per cubic metre
D	electric charge	10	coulomb
E	length	16	metre
F	momentum	14	kilogram metre per second
G	frequency	13	hertz
H	mass	11	kilogram
I	electric current	12	ampere
J	volume	9	cubic metre
K	amount of substance	1	mole
L	force	2	newton
M	time	5	second
N	energy	3	joule
O	stress	15	newton per square metre
P	power	8	watt

SAQ 9 The missing item in each row is as follows:

Row	1	2	3	4	5	6	7	8	9	10
Item	—	10^{-6}	10^{-9}	1 A	1 mm	10^3	1 MHz	1 W	10^{-7}	10^{-15}

Row	11	12	13	14	15	16	17	18	19	20
Item	10^{-3}	10^{-4}	1 GC	10^{-9}	1 nm	1 mN	1 MJ	1 km	10^{-9}	10^9

Perhaps you were caught by row 14. 1 mm = 10^{-3} m, so 1 mm^3 = $(10^{-3})^3$ m^3 = 10^{-9} m^3. You should take particular care with derived units involving squares or cubes of basic units (e.g. area, volume, density, acceleration).

SAQ 10 Both 'base' and height are lengths with the dimension [L]. The dimensions of the right-hand side are therefore [L^2].